Planning
Process Drama

**Pamela Bowell and
Brian S. Heap**

David Fulton Publishers
London

David Fulton Publishers Ltd
The Chiswick Centre, 414 Chiswick High Road, London W4 5TF
www.fultonpublishers.co.uk

First published in Great Britain in 2001 by David Fulton Publishers

Note: The rights of Pamela Bowell and Brian S. Heap to be identified as the authors of this work have been asserted by them in accordance with the Copyright, Designs and Patents Act 1988.

David Fulton Publishers is a division of Granada Learning Limited, part of Granada plc.

British Library Cataloguing in Publication Data
A catalogue record for this book is available from the British Library.

ISBN 1-85346-719-7

Typeset by Elite Typesetting Techniques, Eastleigh, Hampshire
Printed and bound in Great Britain

Contents

Acknowledgements

There are many people to whom acknowledgements are due.

Our thanks go to Dorothy Heathcote, a gifted teacher and pioneer of process drama, whose inspirational work brought us together and set us off down the road; Cecily O'Neill and John O'Toole, who have both contributed to the understanding of process drama; Jonothan Neelands on whose valuable work, in particular his classification of drama strategies, we have drawn; and all those others who have debated and argued with us and encouraged us. Thanks also go to Jan Macdonald and Alayne Ozturk for critically reading drafts of the text and for the many helpful comments and suggestions they have made, and to our respective Heads of Department, Dr Mary Bousted, Head of the School of Education, Kingston University, and Professor the Honourable Rex Nettleford, Vice Chancellor, University of the West Indies, for their invaluable support in enabling us to complete this project.

On a personal level, heartfelt gratitude goes to David and Nicholas Bowell for their years of patience and support and to Philip Palmer for his warmth and hospitality.

Most importantly, thanks go to the drama education students at Kingston University, London, England and at the University of the West Indies, Kingston, Jamaica, who have been our most severe critics and our most ardent supporters.

Preface

This book is about that genre of theatre in an educational setting which is known as process drama. Often called drama in education or 'living through' drama or 'experiential drama', it is the sort of work which is created not for a watching audience but for the benefit of the participants, themselves.

Process drama is to be found in all age phases of school and in the hands of both specialist and non-specialist drama teachers. It is practised in education systems from Britain to New Zealand, from Canada to South Africa, from Finland to Hong Kong, from Jamaica to India; as a discrete subject in its own right or as a cross-curricular methodology.

If you are looking for help to implement process drama with your pupils, then no matter which phase of education you teach, nor which curriculum structure, this book sets out a framework of guiding principles which will enable you to plan process drama to suit your needs and constraints.

We have drawn upon a range of examples, which were originally taught by a number of different teachers. However, for clarity and continuity, we have referred to the teacher as 'she' throughout the text. Similarly, on those occasions when it has been necessary to speak about an individual child we have adopted the convention of 'he'.

While we have referred to numerous examples to illustrate different points in the text, we have introduced three 'key examples' which run throughout. As we discuss each planning principle, the key examples appear so that it is possible to follow through the planning of each drama, seeing how each layer is laid upon the next to build the structure of the drama.

CHAPTER 1

Drama and Education

Key Question:
'Where does drama fit into education?'

Drama within education has had a rather roller-coaster existence. Whether in the UK or other parts of the world, there have been times when it has been valued but there have also been times when it has been out of favour, the victim of a 'back to basics' approach to education.

This situation has been largely politically driven; dependent upon changing governmental opinion about the value of the arts in education. However, in the past, there have also been divisions among some practitioners, themselves, regarding what the precise nature of drama within education should be – a situation which has not always worked to drama's advantage. Fortunately, this situation is giving way, internationally, to a newer climate of consensus.

This is timely. In England, the revised National Curriculum introduced in September 2000, sees drama's role more clearly articulated than it has been for ten years and in other countries such as those of the English-speaking Caribbean, for example, drama has recently achieved a more secure status at all levels of the education system than ever before.

The newly emerging consensus among practitioners recognises an inclusive model of drama within education: a model which seeks to accommodate a range of genres which are all grounded in performance. These will include, for example, opportunities for children to engage in dramatic play, like a dressing up corner in the nursery, perform a classic text, participate in a theatre-in-education programme or share in improvised work in the classroom. What is important, here, is that we understand that *all* these forms of drama experience share the same common elements of theatre: focus, metaphor, tension, symbol, contrast, role, time, space; and, that when, as teachers, we come to plan the drama experiences for the children we teach, no matter in which genre we intend to work, we need to bear these elements in mind.

So, drama experiences in an educational setting can, and, indeed, should, be varied. Teachers need to provide children with the opportunity to engage in a range of challenging, exciting and stimulating drama experiences, grounded in a range of genres, which enable them to understand and manipulate the art form of drama and to use it to develop an understanding of themselves within the world and to comment on their experiences of it.

'But why teach drama in the first place?'

Well, the obvious, short answer for teachers in the United Kingdom and other parts of the world, is 'because the National Curriculum demands it'. However, there are, we believe, more compelling educational reasons which we would like to discuss here as a way of placing this book in the context of children's learning.

We believe that children inhabit the world as fully as adults do – and our task as teachers is to create opportunities which will enable them to interact with that world and to understand it more fully through their interaction so they may function more successfully in it.

However, we recognise that the majority of experiences in school offer children a sort of second-hand interaction with the world, filtered through the teacher, television producer, author and so on. In circumstances such as these, feeling is easily separated from thinking and knowing and when this occurs the chance of information becoming personalised and, therefore, usable knowledge, is reduced. In order to usefully know, we need to feel.

The educationalist, Jerome Bruner, endorsed this view in *Towards a Theory of Instruction*, when he suggested that a learner needs to participate actively in the learning process and that a child's feelings, fantasies and values need to be incorporated into lessons so that knowledge becomes personalised. The drama process makes this possible. By its nature, it affords the chance for first-hand interactive learning experience. In creating a world within a drama and inviting children to invest directly and actively something of themselves in it, the teacher creates the opportunity for understanding to be perceived which is directly transferable to the real world.

'How can this be?'

We realise that on the face of it, this might seem paradoxical. After all, by its nature, drama is make-believe, a fiction, and therefore could be viewed as an escape from reality rather than the reverse! However, to accept this is to ignore the root of the drama process, which is the way in which children make sense of the world around them. That is, through using dramatic play to practise life. The eminent scientist, Jacob Bronowski, in his paper, *The Imaginative Mind in Science*, suggested that 'a child's play frolics in the fantasy world and experiments in the rational world' and that both of these elements are engaged by imagination. It is this unique human ability which enables us all, not just children, to play, to create circumstances which are not actually present to our senses now. This means that we can manipulate images to conjure worlds which are beyond our immediate experiences and by doing this we open the door to all imaginative thought.

The drama process draws upon this natural ability to create imaginary situations through which to explore real experiences: upon our ability to willingly suspend disbelief so that the upturned dining table *is* a sailing ship or the school hall *is* a rainforest when we want them to be. Drama has the ability to link different areas of experience by putting together the faces of fantasy and reality. This enables experiences to illuminate and enrich each other so that changes in perception and understanding can occur. This process provides the opportunity to see afresh and differently.

All children in the course of their dramatic playing project themselves into all worlds, possible and not possible, and by doing so discover for themselves the boundary which lies between them. Imagination actively harnessed within the drama process allows us to see various courses of action, weigh them up and test them out, without suffering the long-term consequences of choice.

If we are parents, early years teachers, have younger siblings or other young children in the family or if we are just keen observers of the behaviour of children, we will all have copious examples of this phenomenon in action. The parent who hears her words of censure echoed when her child plays 'mummies and daddies'; the teacher who sees her own actions recreated in the playground as the children play 'school'; the younger child who creates a situation in which, *this time*, his view prevails instead of that of his older brother or sister.

This is one of the cornerstones on which drama within education is built and, because drama is a social, interactive arts process, it creates experiences which enable the development of cognitive, emotional, social and creative understanding and skills.

'But isn't drama just about acting?'

Of course, one of the important things drama does is give children the opportunity to develop performance skills and perform to others. We mentioned this at the very beginning of this introduction. We also pointed out that performance and the elements of theatre underpin *all* work in drama within an educational context.

However, just as the learning which children gain from involvement in music, dance and the visual arts within education is wide-ranging, so the potential for learning provided by drama is more encompassing than the term 'acting' suggests.

Teachers who are coming newly to drama, especially, may apply too narrow a definition to it and, by so doing, limit the opportunities for their classes.

Drama is empowering. Through the unique process of 'enactment', its diversity of form stimulates creativity and imagination, aesthetic sensitivity and fulfilment. Drama provides opportunities for investigation and reflection, for celebration and challenge. It is a potent means of collaboration and communication which can change the ways people feel, think and behave. By its combination of the affective and the effective, it sharpens perception, enables personal expression and the growth of intellectual and emotional literacy. It provides a framework for the exploration of ideas and feelings and the making of meaning. Drama is embedded in culture and provides a means by which children can understand themselves and relate to those around them.

When teachers create drama opportunities for pupils, they provide a complex, rich and vivid means through which children become artists and, through learning about the art form, develop a means through which to learn about the world around them.

'But how can they learn about drama and about other things through it?'

Well, it is not quite so odd as it sounds. The important thing to realise is that drama always has to have a content. It has to be *about* something. So, it offers children two strands of learning opportunity which are both always present – learning about the nature of drama and learning through drama about other things. It may be that the teacher and/or children decide to focus on one or other at any given moment, but they are both there, always. Perhaps the diagram (Figure 1.1) would help clarify things.

Now let's explain the diagram. A helix is a very good model to explain what we mean. In fact, it has often been used in the past by other practitioners to illustrate the relationship between form and content. It demonstrates quite graphically that the two strands of learning are always there, entwined together. Although one may be in sharper focus than the other at any given moment the other is always present. It also shows that the focus can shift between the two strands. This could be from moment to moment within a drama lesson, or from session to session within a unit of work or from year to year through an entire drama curriculum.

Where the emphasis is on developing theatre skills and an appreciation of theatre, Strand A would obviously be brought to the foreground, but Strand B *must* be present because all theatre has to have a content – it must be about something. Similarly, when the emphasis is on learning about other things through drama, Strand B will be brought into sharper definition. However, if what you are doing is going to be called drama, Strand A *must* be engaged because unless you are using the art form of drama, whatever you are doing, it is *not* drama.

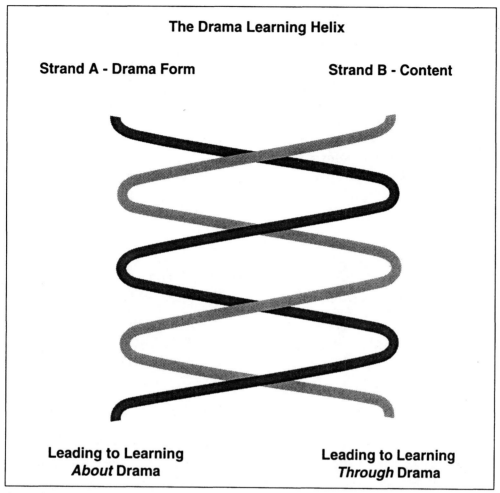

The Drama Learning Helix

Strand A - Drama Form   Strand B - Content

Leading to Learning   Leading to Learning
About Drama   *Through* Drama

Figure 1.1

In staging the wedding scene from Shakespeare's *Much Ado About Nothing* as part of a GCSE drama class, for example, one focus might be on the honing of the performance skills needed to impart the emotional level of the situation. This focus is clearly drawn from what we are calling Strand A. However, in order to discover their characters' motivations and inform their performances, the pupils will need to engage with what this scene of the play is *about*. In fact, it is concerned with jealousy and revenge and, in trying to understand this, therein lies the possibility of examining something of the nature of human relationships – a focus which lies in Strand B.

On the other hand, in a drama with nine-year-olds about the problem of the social costs of traffic congestion in cities – a Strand B focus, the teacher will also be able to press the children, for example, to develop their skills in using a range of drama strategies to present 'evidence' to town planners as effectively as possible – a focus from Strand A.

'So what's this book about?'

As we have already stated, drama within an educational setting encompasses many different genres. However, in our experience, it seems that while teachers value the complete range of approaches, there are some which they find more problematic to structure than others. This leads many to avoid ways of working which they find less easy to implement and yet which have the potential to provide rich and rewarding experiences for children and teacher alike.

What has come to be known as 'process drama' is a case in point and this book seeks to provide a clear guide to the fundamental principles of planning and teaching using this approach.

CHAPTER 2

Distilling the Principles of Planning for Process Drama

Key Question:
'What is process drama?'

Process Drama is a term which has gained greater currency over recent years and is used to describe the genre in which performance to an external audience is absent but presentation to the internal audience is essential. Whereas in some other theatrical genres the meaning is made by the theatrical ensemble of actors, playwright, director and designers and communicated to a *watching* audience; in the genre of process drama the participants, together with the teacher, constitute the theatrical ensemble and engage in drama to make the meaning *for themselves*.

Fundamentally, this is a whole-group drama process, essentially improvised in nature, in which attitude is of greater concern than character. This is not to say that participants in process drama never work in other configurations (they frequently do) nor that they never plan or rehearse aspects of the drama beforehand. However, it is essentially, as the great drama teacher, Dorothy Heathcote, has frequently described it, lived at life-rate and operates from a discovery-at-this-moment basis rather than being memory-based. That is to say that participants in process drama will not normally be involved with learning and presenting lines from a *pre-written* dramatic text – a play – but will be 'writing' their own play as the narrative and tensions of their drama unfold in time and space and through action, reaction and interaction.

It focuses on developing a dramatic response to situations and materials from a range of perspectives. In other words, participants in process drama take on roles that are required for the enquiry, investigation or exploration of the subject matter of the drama. The task of the teacher is to find ways in which to connect the pupils with the content and enable them to develop responses to it through active engagement and reflection.

By privileging the participants' ability to empathise and respond to a situation or given materials, the way is open for the teacher to introduce a range of dramatic strategies which will lead to deeper engagement with the subject matter of the drama while, at the same time, broadening the participants' experience of the conventions of the art form and their ability to creatively manipulate them for themselves.

'What do children learn through process drama?'

Practitioners have described the areas of learning in drama in a number of different ways but most agree that the learning falls into broad categories which include:

- learning about the art form;
- personal and social learning – including language, moral and spiritual development; and,
- cross-curricular learning.

If we refer again to the helix diagram of learning strands, it is easy to see how the areas of learning relate to the strands. Strand A subsumes the learning about the art form area and Strand B subsumes the cross-curricular and personal and social areas.

It is important that we recognise this broad scope for learning inherent within engagement with drama because such recognition will enable us as teachers to plan drama experiences for children which provide optimum potential for that learning to take place.

The most important aspect to keep in mind is that, no matter which learning objectives we have set for the children – personal and social, cross-curricular or about the art form – the *absolutely* most effective way of ensuring that the children achieve them is to plan the best drama experience possible. In a nutshell, the better the drama, the better the learning.

The better we can make the process drama experience for the children through our careful planning, preparation and delivery, the greater will be the learning about the art form of drama and about other areas of the curriculum through drama. But, good drama, if it is to be effective, like any other educational activity, requires serious planning.

'Are there any guiding principles to planning good process drama?'

Process drama rests on a number of cornerstones. We have already identified one in the preceding chapter – the innate predisposition of children to learn through dramatic playing. There are others, also, as you can see in the diagram (Figure 2.1), that we need to identify and keep in mind as they *underpin* the planning of the drama: a recognition that learning takes place most effectively when it is contextualised; that learners who have a sense of ownership about their learning have a greater commitment to it and therefore gain more from it as a result and that, universally, human beings use drama to symbolically represent life experiences and to make comment on them. These all have a direct bearing upon the planning of process drama.

Crucially, each informs the nature of the learning structures we create with the children and impact upon the place of the teacher within them. As this book unfolds, we will return to each of these in greater detail but now we wish to turn to the principles of planning process drama.

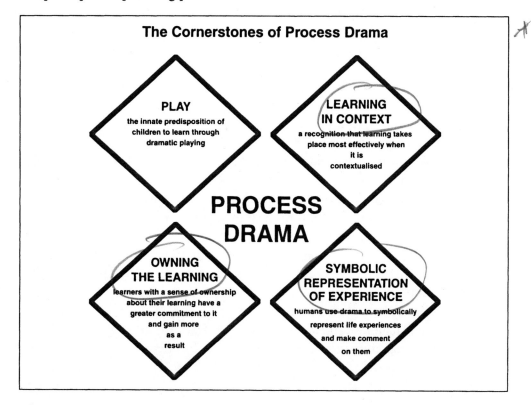

Figure 2.1

The principles of planning

Drama, like any other subject, needs to be planned with rigour if the teacher is to provide the best opportunity for the pupils to learn. Our experience over many years, has led us to the conclusion that the principles of planning process drama remain constant whether planning for five-year-olds, 15-year-olds or, indeed, any age of learner. So, the rest of this chapter sets out an overview of what we consider to be the key principles of planning for process drama which, we believe, will help you no matter in what age phase of education you teach.

These planning principles are namely:
1. theme/learning area
2. context
3. roles
4. frame
5. sign
6. strategies.

Perhaps it would be useful here to say something which will help to clarify our terminology. We mentioned in the opening chapter that all forms of drama experience share the same common elements of theatre, including focus, metaphor, role, tension, symbol, contrast, time and space. If we are planning a process drama therefore, we have to ensure that what we build is scaffolded by these structural elements. The six principles of planning we have named here and their implementation, which is at the heart of this book, are the means by which we construct the drama and ensure that the elements of theatre are incorporated.

So let's look in a little more detail at each of them here. This will be a brief introduction in which we can see how the principles of planning and the elements of theatre relate to each other. When we revisit each planning principle in its own dedicated chapter, we will be exploring each in greater detail.

1. Theme/Learning Area

We've already stated that drama must be about something. It must have a content. This is actually what the theatre element 'focus' refers to. It is the *particular* aspect of the human condition under examination in the drama. In the educational setting, this focus or content will most likely be drawn from the broad curriculum as themes and topics or from the cross-curricular issues such as personal and social development. It is from these themes, topics or issues that the focus of the drama will be distilled, so that in process drama, we can say that the theatre element of 'focus' is created through the choice of theme or learning area.

2. Context

In order to explore the theme or learning area on which we have decided to focus, we will need to develop a dramatic context. This dramatic context provides the particular *fictional* circumstances in which the theme will be explored. Essentially, as a fiction – the dramatic context *stands for* the real life human experience which will be explored in the drama. In other words, the dramatic context is the theatrical element of metaphor.

3. Roles

Another fundamental element of theatre and central to all performance forms is the taking of a role. In this aspect, the relationship between the planning principles and theatre elements is most obvious, because they share the same terminology.

4. Frame

Tension is the theatre element which 'charges' the drama. In planning for process drama, frame is a term we have used to describe the tension-giver. Frame provides the means by which competing protagonistic and antagonistic forces, that is to say those characters or agencies in the drama who are in conflict about the outcome of the central dilemma, are introduced. In our view, planning an effective frame is the most crucial principle of all. While frame is a term borrowed from sociology, nevertheless, we would argue that it admirably suits the social nature of the art form.

5. Sign (_cotton_)

An intricate system of signs, including objects, sounds, language, gestures and images combine in all theatre genres to bring significance to the events of the drama and direct attention to them. Signs represent more than just their utilitarian function. As we have established, dramas are metaphors for life experience and, within this framework, signs are the means by which the theatre element of symbol is evoked. The crucial aspect of signs, therefore, is that they function symbolically and efficiently. This means that organisation for significance is a fundamental principle for planning process drama.

6. Strategies

These are ways of working based on performance forms which bring the drama into life. In recognising that action in space and time are the elements which make theatre a dynamic form, strategies enable us to make adjustments to each. Moreover, using a range of strategies supports the element of contrast in the drama. This is important because drama hinges on three sets of contrasts – silence and sound, stillness and movement and darkness and light. Strategies which allow us to adjust time, space and contrasts help meaning to be made through the friction at the interface between them. In process drama terms, the judicious use of a range of strategies, therefore, enables teacher and pupils to explore time, place and event from different perspectives.

'This seems like a lot to take in'

We know that this may sound a bit daunting but we hope that as the book unfolds you will see how these principles and elements relate to each other and how it is possible for even a quite inexperienced teacher to get to grips with the planning of high quality process drama with confidence.

Let's move on by seeing, in Figure 2.2, how the planning principles relate to each other. If you remember that by following these principles of planning you will be building in the necessary theatre elements to your drama, then what we need to do now is look at the questions the teacher needs to ask herself in order to help her plan.

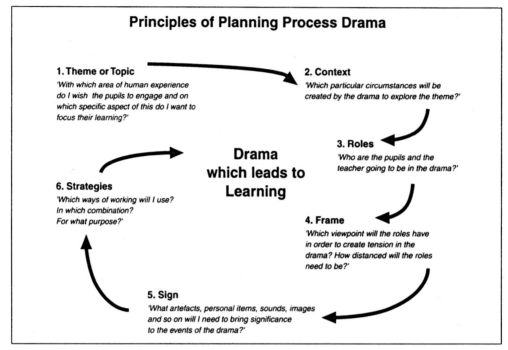

Figure 2.2

You can see in the diagram that each of the planning principles can be presented in terms of a series of key questions which the teacher must answer. So, we are going to look at each of the principles and, this time, explore the key questions for each.

1.   Theme/Learning Area *'With which area of human experience do I wish the pupils to engage and on which specific aspect of this do I want to focus their learning?'*

Just as with every other curriculum area or subject, it is essential from the beginning of the planning process for the teacher to identify precisely what her learning objectives for the class are. Particularly in the present climate of increased accountability in education, teachers need to clearly identify what *precisely* they wish pupils to gain from each lesson so that they can make informed decisions about how best to plan for that learning to take place. Moreover, because process drama is always concerned with matters of human significance, the teacher will also need to define the theme or learning area in terms of the human dimension within it.

2.   Context *'Which particular circumstances will be created by the drama to explore the theme?'*

The answer to the first question will often be in a broad, abstract or conceptual form. However, in order for the children to engage with the theme, the teacher needs to present it in a concrete form and within a defined framework made up of a carefully selected place, time and situation in which the action of the drama can unfold. An appropriately chosen dramatic context will offer the fictional circumstances in which pupils have the opportunity to thoroughly explore the theme in a meaningful way.

3. Roles *'Who are the pupils and the teacher going to be in the drama?'*
The fundamental activity in drama is taking on a role – imagining that you are someone else and exploring a situation through that person's eyes. Having selected a dramatic context – the fictional circumstances of the drama – the teacher will now need to 'people' it by deciding upon the roles – the people – that the children are going to become in the drama. She will need to ensure that those she chooses are found in the time and place of the context and will have an appropriate 'reason' for engaging with the theme. Because teacher-in-role is a fundamental aspect of process drama, the teacher will also have to decide on which role she is going to take in the drama.

4. Frame *'Which viewpoint will the roles have in order to create tension in the drama and how distanced will the roles need to be?'*
The currency of process drama is talk, and so creating the climate in which meaningful talk can be generated is a key element of planning. In process drama it is the point of view which the role has about what is happening in the drama which is critical in generating this climate. It gives the participants something to talk about. One aspect of frame provides the dramatic tension necessary to drive the drama forward – the communication frame.

There is a second aspect of frame which is concerned with what Dorothy Heathcote calls 'protecting into the experience'. Often in drama we want participants to engage with sensitive or difficult material or with situations which are far beyond their own immediate experience. In circumstances like these we need to find a framework which will enable participation safely. Application of the second aspect of frame allows this to happen – it is known as the distancing frame.

5. Sign *'What artefacts, personal items, sounds, images and so on will I need to bring significance to the events?'*
When planning a process drama, we deliberately set out to create an exciting, stimulating learning experience for our pupils which will engage them on a number of levels. We do this, however, with a clear learning outcome in mind, and so need to ensure that in the midst of such an experience, the pupils' attention is directed to the heart of the learning. One of the key ways this happens is through the use of signs. These are things such as artefacts and personal items – documents, images and three-dimensional objects for instance – which bring significance to the drama, direct the children's attention and help them to explore actively the precise focus of the lesson.

6. Strategies *'Which ways of working will I use? In which combination? For what purpose?'*

There are many different ways of creating the drama, of making it happen, moving it forward and enabling reflection on what has happened in it and contemplation of what is to come. An informed choice of strategies, by the teacher who recognises their different qualities, will provide pupils with the opportunity to learn about the art form and will also provide them with the means to explore and present the content of the drama and to reflect upon it.

'Can you say more about these principles in detail?'

Yes. It is important now to explore each of the principles in more depth so that the way in which they relate to each other and combine to produce a powerful process drama can be seen more clearly. Therefore, in subsequent chapters, we will examine each principle in closer detail.

As you work through the planning sequence and, especially as you become more familiar with what to do, you will find that, often, ideas will overlap, pop into your mind simultaneously or in a different order to the one we are setting out here. However, to make sure that we pay sufficient attention to each principle, so that we explain them clearly, we are going to deal with each one separately by setting them out in a linear sequence. Moreover, if you are new to process drama, following this sequence, step by step, will help you to understand and plan successfully.

What follows next, then, is the chapter dealing with the first principle, and this is the one which always comes first – deciding the theme or learning area.

CHAPTER 3

Theme/Learning Area

Key Question:
'With which area of human experience do I want the pupils to engage?'

While there will always be unexpected outcomes, learning through process drama is not arbitrary or random. In determining a theme for drama, whether she is a generalist primary teacher or a drama specialist in secondary school, the most important question for the teacher to ask is '*what do I want the children to learn about?*' What is the focus of the drama?

We have already considered that when pupils are engaged in drama, the nature of the experience means that they will have the opportunity for learning in three broad categories – learning about the art form of drama itself, personal and social learning, and cross-curricular learning. If the teacher bears these in mind, they will help her to find the answer to the very important question she has asked herself. The result should be an *informed* choice of theme or learning area for the drama.

So, for example:

personal and social learning
  – do the pupils need to work more effectively in a team?
  – do they need to enhance their self-esteem?
  – do they need to have a greater connection to the local community?
  – do they need to understand how people have dealt with racism?

learning about the art form
  – do they need to work on drama using space and levels?
  – do they need to be able to express themselves more physically?
  – do they need to use more dialogue and use voice more expressively?
  – which new strategies do I want to introduce to the class?

cross-curricular learning
- do they need to learn about the great contribution of women in the First World War?
- do they need to know about the worldwide achievement of the West Indies in sports, art and culture, music, science and technology, public life, medicine, etc?
- do they need to explore the impact of global warming on world climate?

Asking ourselves such questions will help begin to focus in on what we want pupils to learn from the drama and will also put us in a position to make informed decisions in planning the experience for the class.

'But what about prescribed curricula?'

Many teachers find themselves working within the constraints of what variously might be called a state, a provincial or a national curriculum. In these circumstances, the scope of drama may well be contained by these prescribed curricula so that our practice is shaped by what is laid down by local or national authority. In effect, for some teachers, this may mean they have a very broad range of possibilities from which to work. For others, opportunities will need to be found from within a much narrower and more closely defined spectrum of activity.

Let's look at an example. In England, the revised National Curriculum, published by the Department for Education and Employment and introduced in September 2000, has articulated Drama's place more clearly than has ever been the case.

At present, it remains subsumed within the broad National Curriculum for English, but the revised version gives greater prominence to drama than its predecessors. Although reference is made to drama in both the Reading and Writing Programmes of Study and in the National Literacy Strategy, the greatest emphasis lies within the Speaking and Listening Programmes of Study and what follows is a summary of its contents.

Drama in the National Curriculum for England 2000

Key Stage 1
During Key Stage 1 pupils 'learn to use language in imaginative ways and express their ideas and feelings when working in role and in drama activities'.

En1 Speaking and Listening
Knowledge, Skills and Understanding
'Drama
4   To participate in a range of drama activities, pupils should be taught to:
    (a) use language and actions to explore and convey situations, characters and emotions
    (b) create and sustain roles individually and when working with others
    (c) comment constructively on drama they have watched or in which they have taken part.'

Breadth of Study
'Drama Activities
11 The range should include:
    (a) working in role
    (b) presenting drama and stories to others (for example, telling a story through tableaux or using a narrator)
    (c) responding to performances.'

Key Stage 2
En1 Speaking and Listening
Knowledge, Skills and Understanding
'Drama
4   To participate in a wide range of drama activities and to evaluate their own and others' contributions, pupils should be taught to:
    (a) create, adapt and sustain different roles, individually and in groups
    (b) use character, action and narrative to convey story, themes, emotions, ideas in plays they devise and script
    (c) use dramatic techniques to explore characters and issues (for example, hot seating, flashback)
    (d) evaluate how they and others have contributed to the overall effectiveness of performances.'

Breadth of Study
'Drama Activities

11   The range should include:

(a) improvisation and working in role

(b) scripting and performing in plays

(c) responding to performances.'

Key Stages 3 and 4
En1 Speaking and Listening
Knowledge, Skills and Understanding
'Drama

4   To participate in a range of drama activities and to evaluate their own and others' contributions, pupils should be taught to:

(a) use a variety of dramatic techniques to explore ideas, issues, texts and meanings

(b) use different ways to convey action, character, atmosphere and tension when they are scripting and performing in plays (for example, through dialogue, movement, pace)

(c) appreciate how the structure and organisation of scenes and plays contribute to dramatic effect

(d) evaluate critically performances of dramas that they have watched or in which they have taken part.'

Breadth of Study
'Drama Activities

11   The range should include:

(a) improvisation and working in role

(b) devising, scripting and performing in plays

(c) discussing and reviewing their own and others' performances.'

If we look at another example, this time from Jamaica, the curriculum for Grades 1–9 contains the following.

Jamaican Drama Curriculum

Grades 1–3 Integrated Primary Curriculum

The Integrated Primary Curriculum is built around 'All about Me and My Environment' and incorporates **'The Aesthetics in the Primary Curriculum'**.

(a) Drama

(b) Visual Arts

(c) Music

(d) Movement Education and Dance

Drama activities for Grades 1–3 include:

(a) acting out roles (from stories and other sources)

(b) simple mime activities

(c) action songs and rhymes

(d) improvising simple situations

Drama Curriculum for Grades 4–6

Grade 4 Drama Units

(a) Story Building

(b) Creative Use of Movement

(c) Exploring the Senses

Grade 5 Drama Units

(a) Inventive Role Play

(b) Creating Dramatic Narrative

(c) Exploring Voice for Dramatic Performance

Grade 6 Drama Units

(a) Creating the Play through Process

(b) Culture and Drama

(c) Establishing Relationships within the Drama

Grades 4–6 Drama activities include:

(a) capturing the theme of a story in tableaux

(b) acting out a story using mime

(c) taking a role

(d) using improvisation to explore specific ideas or problems

(e) using role-play activities to deal with interpersonal relations or problem-solving

Drama Curriculum for Grades 7–9

Grade 7 Drama

Exploration Year

(a) The Individual Instrument – discovering personal, physical and vocal skills and potential

(b) Making and Maintaining Contact – sharing stories and experiences in pairs and small groups

(c) The Individual and the Group – playing your part in the larger group

Grade 8 Drama
Development Year
   (a) Building Characters – from externals to inner life
   (b) Portraying Relationships – showing how characters behave toward one another
   (c) What's the Plot? – the arrangement of incidents

Grade 9 Drama
Interpretation Year
   (a) What's in the Script? – context, tension, focus, space and time
   (b) Making it Mean Something – language, movement, mood, meaning, symbol
   (c) Putting It All Together – improvisation or text into performance

'I'm not sure I understand what this means I have to do'

With the constantly changing shape of national curricula, teachers in many situations, especially primary school teachers, are finding themselves faced with having to teach some things with which they are less familiar or less confident. Given that our individual training experiences are different, then it is not surprising that some teachers, perhaps, will be a bit daunted when faced with a drama curriculum.

However, it seems to us that the content of most drama curricula can be broken down into a number of *broad* categories:

- creating drama – including investigation, experimentation and responding to stimuli;
- presenting drama; and,
- responding to/critically reflecting upon drama.

Looked at in this way, what is prescribed becomes more manageable and, although some might see this as an over-simplification and others may well use alternative categories, we think that this breakdown is a helpful one for teachers coming newly to the teaching of drama.

If we think about this a bit more, it becomes clear that experience of process drama is one among a range of genres which the teacher may well need to offer to pupils if their curriculum is going to be delivered effectively. By looking in more detail at how to structure process drama experiences for pupils, as we shall be in following chapters, and by following through a number of key examples, we will be able to see, also, how this particular genre of theatre provides opportunity to meet curricular requirements.

But there are also other key cross-curricular themes which many teachers are required to address, such as Personal, Social and Health Education, the spiritual, moral and cultural dimensions of the curriculum, citizenship and creativity. Here, process drama offers a dynamic, effective and affective means through which pupils can engage with these important issues. This is because *the social interaction of human beings and the exploration of issues which are significant to them, lie at the heart of all drama.*

'But already there's not enough time to fit everything in. How can we add drama?'

No matter where we teach, it seems certainly true that we have ever greater demands placed upon us. In curricula which are crowded there is a real concern about how teachers can ensure that each subject is given due attention. Under circumstances like these, especially in those situations in which drama does not stand as a discrete subject, then finding the time for it can be difficult.

However, if we look at this problem from another point of view, we can perhaps see another way to make time available.

We have already pointed out that process drama, as all drama, must have a content, it has to be *about something.* We've already suggested that cross-curricular themes lend themselves to exploration through drama. But, in addition to this, we can also look to the curriculum content of other subjects as a source of material. Exploring this through drama will provide exciting and engaging opportunities to enhance pupils' learning about that content *and* also provide time in which they can continue to develop their ability to use the drama form, just as we illustrated in the diagram about learning Strands A and B in Chapter 1. So, providing that when we choose the subject matter we remember that drama is always concerned with *people*, with matters concerned with the human condition, then the scope for drama within the whole curriculum is really very broad.

'Does drama really always have to be about people and the human condition?'

Actually, yes. It is absolutely essential to remember that drama is concerned with *people and their life experiences.* [Drama, like all art forms, is concerned with the symbolic representation of life experience and this is compounded by its being a social, interactive arts process – *drama is essentially about people and their relationships, dilemmas, concerns, hopes, fears, aspirations, celebrations and rites of passage*, all of which create ties which bind them together.]

So, when choosing the learning area, we need to identify some aspect of the human condition to learn about. This seems relatively straightforward if, for example, the teacher is embarking on an examination of 'racism' or 'friendship' or *The Diary of Anne Frank*, which all obviously deal with some aspect of human experience.

However, if something like 'transport' is the class theme (which may well be the case in a primary or elementary school, for example) then we must ask how 'people' and 'transport' go together. The teacher needs to tease out the human dimension because, while little learning about the topic will come from pupils pretending to be cars or trains, a great deal will come from their considering, in role, the dilemma of new roads disrupting old communities or the dichotomy between the benefits of air travel and the accompanying noise pollution.

Teachers often see traditional tales such as *Goldilocks and the Three Bears*, the Anansi stories of West Africa and the Caribbean; or *Aesop's Fables*, all of which feature animals as central characters, as a potentially rich source of drama. This is, indeed, true. However, dramas based on such stories will only succeed if we remember that they work metaphorically and actually reflect the human condition and not the behaviour of animals. So in dramas based on stories like these, even when pupils take on the role of animals, they will need to be focused on the resolving of the human-like dilemmas which face them rather than 'acting' like animals.

Again, if the teacher really thinks about it, even a learning area like 'seismology' has within it the potential for drama provided it is approached from the point of view of the impact of nature upon people. For example, the impact of earthquakes and volcanoes on different civilisations, the dilemma between the need to enforce strict building codes and the demand of people for cheap housing in an earthquake zone, or the dilemma of those who farm the nutrient-rich soils on active volcanic slopes but who are at daily risk from an eruption.

'Could you give some more detailed examples?'

This might be a good point at which to introduce a set of three key examples that we will be developing and to which we will be returning at each stage in the book as the planning process unfolds.

Key Example 1 – 6/7-year-olds

Theme/Learning Area
taking plant species from an environment
impacts negatively on the local people

Background
A class of 30 mixed ability 6- and 7-year-olds in an inner city infant school in London. This was a lively class of pupils who had some previous experience of process drama. The drama took place within the classroom, with tables moved

back when appropriate and was taught in five weekly, one-hour sessions, combining timetabled time for science and drama. This was because the hall was unavailable at the time needed.

Reasons for selecting theme
Under the Science National Curriculum Attainment Targets 1 and 2, the teacher wished to use process drama to enhance the pupils' investigative skills and develop their appreciation of the need to care for living things in their environment. She also wished them to develop their skills of collaboration, decision-making and problem-solving. Finally, she wished to broaden their knowledge of drama strategies by using ways of working which the pupils had not yet met. This theme – *taking plant species from an environment impacts negatively on the local people* – offered the potential for developing a process drama which had, at its heart, a human dimension in the shape of a conflict of interests.

Key Example 2 – 8/9-year-olds

Theme/Learning Area
what makes human beings give up
what they know and take a long and difficult
journey in the hope of something better at the end?

Background
A class of 32 mixed ability 8- and 9-year-olds in an inner-city primary school in London with a particularly rich ethnic and cultural mix. This was also a lively class of pupils who had some experience of process drama. The drama, for the most part, took place in the hall and was taught over ten, weekly 45-minute sessions, combining timetabled time for Personal, Social and Health Education (PHSE) and for English.

Reasons for choice of theme
The children's own family backgrounds were very diverse. The overwhelming majority came from families which had relocated to London from a range of places, both intra- and inter-nationally. In order to explore and celebrate this situation and to respond to elements of the PHSE and Citizenship curriculum requirements, the teacher decided on this theme – *what makes human beings give up what they know and take a long and difficult journey in the hope of something better at the end?* Dramatically, this also held the potential to draw upon the archetypal narrative structure of 'the journey'.

Key Example 3 – 11/13-year-olds

Theme/Learning Area
creation theory versus evolution theory – why does a tension
exist between those who hold different views about
the origins of life on earth?

Background
A group of 35 Jamaican able and talented 11- to 13-year-olds, selected from
different schools to participate in a workshop held over five consecutive days.
Some of the students involved were developing behavioural problems associated
with the fact that their current scheme of work in school was insufficiently
challenging and was uninteresting. One of the aims of the workshop was to help
teachers and parents of the children understand the need to develop
supplementary enrichment programmes.

Reasons for choice of theme
The brief given to the teacher by the organisers of the workshop was to use drama
with a science-based theme which could readily accommodate a range of creative
and artistic expression, visits by resource persons from the community, and
culminating in a presentation of work to parents, teachers and friends. A high level
of ability among the pupils also meant that the theme selected, while relating to
the existing curriculum, would have to be more challenging, motivating the
students to fully engage their intellectual capabilities. It was further felt that the
controversial nature of a theme like *creation theory versus evolution theory – why does
a tension exist between those who hold different views about the origins of life on earth?*
– might stimulate a high level of debate and discussion. There was also a need to
encourage greater self-motivation in the participants, and therefore, a need to
develop an authentic research atmosphere in which the task-oriented dramatic
activity could take place.

   We hope that it is clear from our three key examples that the teacher needs to be
sure about what she wishes to teach the pupils through process drama and that she
must hold in mind, always, that the drama must have human interaction at its
centre.

'Are there any other considerations regarding choice of theme?'

At first glance, the contents of some prescribed curricula may not readily appear to
lend themselves to exploration through drama. Sometimes they appear to be too
general or too academic to inspire any real creativity in the approach to their
delivery. However, all curricula address at least *some* aspects of human experience

and this is the key to bringing drama and the rest of the curriculum together to enable children's learning. Broad themes can be broken down into a range of topics and sub-topics in a way which will eventually reveal the human dimension and so yield their potential for exploration through drama and we shall talk about this in greater detail, shortly. However, we also need to bear in mind that other constraints impact upon planning and factors such as time, space and availability of resources have to be given serious consideration, too.

The availability of resources needs to be borne in mind. We have to be sure that the learning area for the drama chosen by the teacher can be supported by the appropriate materials and information. The process drama approach to learning often creates an imperative for research, manufacture and creative endeavour – in fact, this is one of its many strengths. The teacher therefore needs to be able to provide what the pupils need. For example, if the teacher chooses to do a drama in which the pupils will be required to create illuminated manuscripts then clearly she needs to be able to provide paper and markers at the very least. Or, if the drama demands that the pupils make a variety of sound effects, then the teacher will need to provide the means by which these can be made. This does not imply that a teacher needs to have a stock cupboard full of paper or musical instruments before she can plan for drama; imagination can create much of what is needed. However, in a drama with particular tasks at its heart which demand that the pupils actually undertake them (such as creating manuscripts), if those sorts of resources are in short supply then the drama should be about something else!

Yet another critical consideration in choosing a theme for drama is the amount and type of space that the teacher has at her disposal. Many teachers automatically think that in order to teach a drama session they need access to a large, open space such as the school hall or a drama studio. However, in practice, much high quality drama can take place in the ordinary classroom environment. This does not mean that a large space might not be desirable, even crucial, for some sections of a drama but it does mean that if it's not available, then with a judicious choice of theme, the teacher can create a drama with her class which is positively enhanced by taking place within the classroom where chairs, tables and writing materials, for example, are available.

In other words, as a teacher you need to cut your coat according to your cloth! And on an encouraging note, we want to stress that some of the most creative and educative drama is born out of situations which have the fewest resources.

'What comes next?'

We have now reached a point where the teacher is clear about the learning area for the drama. However, this is still in an abstract or conceptual form. The teacher now needs to decide which *particular set of circumstances* will be created in the fiction of the drama to explore the theme in a concrete way. So, in the following chapter we will consider what the teacher needs to do in order to choose the dramatic context and will be using a range of examples, including our key examples, to illustrate the points we are making.

CHAPTER 4

Context

**Key Question:
'Which particular circumstances will be created by the drama to explore the theme?'**

The term 'context' is frequently used in drama. It is a key notion but one which is complex because, in reality, the same word is used to refer to several different, but important, *sorts* of circumstances.

Other practitioners have written extensively about the different contexts in drama but we are going to highlight just three aspects of context in relation to drama and concentrate on the one we feel teachers new to process drama find most difficult to define – that is the *dramatic* context.

'Could you explain what you mean by these different aspects of context?'

It's not really very complicated. Let's start with the one with which we will all be most familiar, *the real life context*.

Education does not happen in a vacuum. As teachers, we all know that we need to take many different circumstances into consideration when planning learning experiences for the pupils we teach: their age, gender, experience, the social health of the group, the culture and ethos of the school, the place in which the drama is to happen, the curriculum demands and so on. These considerations have a bearing on the planning of process drama, too, and the teacher will have had them in the forefront of her mind when choosing the theme or learning area she wishes the pupils to tackle in the drama. When you come to plan process drama for yourself you will bring your own clear knowledge and understanding of all these circumstances to the choices you make in planning the drama for your class.

For example, if you have a confined space in which to work, then planning a drama which demands a great deal of physical activity in a lot of space would not be appropriate; if you have a class for whom the language of instruction is not their mother tongue, this too will impact on the choice of subject matter and structure of the drama; if you are inexperienced in teaching drama, you might wish to start with a more simple, one-lesson drama rather than one which runs on over a number of sessions; if there has been an instance of bullying in the class, creating a piece of drama which explores the issue analogously will be much more appropriate than one in which the child who has been bullied is placed in a vulnerable position.

Let's now look at the second sort of 'context' which impacts on process drama – *the need for learning to have a context.*

Educational research, such as the work of Margaret Donaldson in her book, *Children's Minds*, has underlined what we as teachers already know from our experience – that is, that learning takes place most effectively when it is contextualised. While we are able, on occasion, to change the learning context for pupils – a visit to the museum, theatre, fire station, for example; with the best will in the world, time and financial constraints usually mean that for delivering the greatest part of the school curriculum, there is only one basic context for learning – that is, pupils in the classroom with the teacher.

However, there is a way in which we can access an infinite variety of contexts for learning – without leaving the school. This, of course, is through imagination in action – drama. As we have already stressed, children naturally use dramatic playing as a way of learning about the world in which they live. They naturally place themselves in imagined roles or places and by this procedure explore the 'what if' of a wide range of situations so as to understand them better.

Children's ability to 'willingly suspend disbelief' and imagine themselves into an infinite variety of experiences is one of the foundations upon which process drama rests. It allows the teacher to harness the pupils' creative energy in order to *contextualise* the learning that she wants for them.

For example, children's language learning takes place and develops through interactions in meaningful circumstances which suit the context in which the language is required. Process drama can create an infinite range of meaningful circumstances which provide just such opportunities for different modes of language, both verbal and written, to be used in context. We know, of course, that these circumstances are *fictional*, but because of the children's suspension of disbelief, they become, for the duration of the drama, '*real*'.

Furthermore, drama engages children on a cognitive, kinaesthetic and *emotional* level. Coupled with their suspension of disbelief, this means that children find a 'real' reason in the drama for doing a host of activities – researching, problem-solving, negotiating, writing, building relationships and so on, because they *care* about the outcome of the drama. When, so often, children in school do things simply because the teacher requires them to, drama becomes a powerful means by which the teacher can help them to construct an imperative for learning, *for themselves* – what Dorothy Heathcote, in the video, *Pieces of Dorothy*, calls 'education for self-direction'. Of course, as teachers we will always need to require children to do a host of things as part of their learning activities in school. However, if a teacher recognises the power which drama has to *motivate* learning by engaging children at the *affective* as well as cognitive level then she has at her disposal the means to aid the development of the whole child.

'This is a bit complicated, could you give a practical example?'

Well, here is an example from a drama with a class of six-year-olds in London, around the theme of non-standard units of measurement. The children, as villagers, developed a very real concern about the giant's sore feet and the need to make him a pair of sandals. To achieve this, they were precipitated into using non-standard units of measurement – their own hand spans, feet and so on, in order to carry out the vital task of measuring the size of the giant's feet. This they did with a rigour and application which was born out of the sense of purpose provided by the fictional context of the drama.

In this instance, the drama contextualised learning about the mathematical concept of non-standard units of measurement through a cognitive, kinaesthetic and *emotional* engagement with the material. It provided the children with a 'real' reason for using hand spans and such, and the multifaceted nature of the experience maximised their opportunity to *remember* what they had done and to feel good about what they had achieved.

As we said a moment ago, drama contextualises learning in fictional circumstances. If a teacher is convinced by drama's ability to do this, then she needs to be able to plan these circumstances, or *dramatic contexts*, in which the learning can take place. This is the third aspect of context that we wish to explore. It is directly connected to the choice the teacher has made about what she wants the children to learn about, that is the theme or learning area, which we discussed in the previous chapter.

The selection of a particular set of fictional circumstances is the first big test for the teacher in planning process drama. She must develop the skill to translate what may be a general, broad or even abstract theme into a *concrete* situation in which the participants can interact in a meaningful way. In other words, she has to choose an appropriate *dramatic context* in which to explore the theme.

'How do I go about choosing an appropriate dramatic context?'

The success of your choice will depend on your ability to tightly define *exactly* what you want the children to learn about. If, for example, you had chosen 'The Vikings' as the learning area for a Key Stage 2/Upper Primary class, you might be tempted to think that you have decided enough to move on to the choice of dramatic context. However, 'The Vikings' is actually too loose a definition to allow for clear planning. It is not focused. A teacher is unlikely to plan a successful history lesson, for example, with such an unfocused learning goal. She will ask herself 'what exactly about the Vikings do I want the children to learn about today?' and plan her lesson accordingly. So it is with planning process drama. The *exact* nature of the learning you want to promote will lead you into a range of dramatic contexts which will allow that learning to take place.

If we follow the Viking example, we need to decide what, *precisely*, it is about the Vikings that you want the children to learn in the drama. It isn't sufficient to say 'we're going to do a drama about the Vikings' – the teacher needs to identify *exactly what* about the Vikings she wants the children to engage with; for example, the navigation skills of the Vikings, the social structure of the Vikings and its consequences, the Vikings as artists, the Vikings as warriors, the Viking myths and legends, Viking settlements and occupations, the effect of the Vikings on other peoples, the Anglo-Saxon response to the Viking invasion.

'But the possibilities seem endless!'

Let's take an example. Having narrowed down the focus of enquiry from the general topic of The Vikings to a more specific aspect such as how the Anglo-Saxons responded to the Viking invasion, then it is possible to think of a range of *dramatic contexts* in which this might be explored.

Place	Time period	Event
Holy Island	Viking times	the Viking landing
mainland village	Viking times	preparing to repel the invaders
monastery	Mediaeval times	chronicling Viking invasion
village	modern times	commemorating defence of village
film studio	modern times	making a film about the invasion
archaeological site	modern times	excavating site of battle
museum	modern times	setting up living museum display

and many more

Now a choice has to be made from this list. This might seem overwhelming at first but it is really a situation which should actually be seen as advantageous. In effect it means that the teacher has leeway to select the context which will most suit and benefit the particular class of children for whom the drama is being planned.

Therefore, multiple dramatic contexts are available to you as a teac
offering a different handle on desired learning outcomes. You jus
remember that no context is necessarily better than another. They all si...
different possibilities to the children.

'So how can you tell what kind of dramatic context will be most appropriate for a particular class of children?'

This is where the *real life context* informs your thinking about the dramatic
context. Because each class has its own particular strengths and weaknesses, mix of
personalities and needs, culturally specific curriculum and ethnic and gender mix,
what seems to be a good choice for one group will not necessarily be at all
appropriate for another. But the idea of focusing the learning area in order to get
to the dramatic context remains the same. As we can see from the Viking example,
there are basically three steps:

Step 1:   decide exactly what you want the children to learn about the theme;
Step 2:   think of as many dramatic contexts as possible in which it might be explored;
Step 3:   choose the one which best suits the children for whom it is intended.

'Could we try it with another example?'

Let's take something which is not necessarily historically-based and at the same
time is broad and universal, for example, Water.

Step 1:   exactly what do I want the children to learn about water?

> *Water is a precious commodity and we need to conserve it*

Step 2:   how many contexts can I think of in which this could be explored?

Place	Time period	Event
plant nursery	present day	finding ways to reduce water costs
hospital	present day	devising systems for recycling waste water
mountain forest	present day	preventing lowland flooding created by deforestation
desert oasis	present day	calculating water needed to get caravan across the desert
village community	present day	designing ways of storing water for use in dry season
life raft after plane wreck at sea	present day	deciding how to collect portable water to stay alive
polluted river	present day	experimentation with natural means to decontaminate water such as water hyacinths

and many more

Step 3:   choose the one which best fits the children for whom it is intended.

Class: Year 5 (9 to 10-year-olds) in Kingston, Jamaica.

Real Life Context: Water is a critical issue in Jamaica, the pupils regularly wasted water by failing to turn off water in school wash basins. Children had difficulty in seeing consequences of this negligence. Teacher judged that a dramatic context was needed which brought home to them (a) water has a cost and (b) without water, things die.

Dramatic Context: From brainstormed list above, the plant nursery was chosen by the teacher as the context which would most suit this class because growing plants would most immediately bring home to the children the consequences of actions.

It is important to say again that this choice did *not* mean that the other possible contexts offered poorer learning opportunities *per se.* They offered a range of lenses through which to examine the desired learning but the one chosen, in the opinion of the teacher, was most appropriate for the particular class.

It is also important to point out that each would have given a different *slant* on the chosen theme. They would have all addressed the issue but the learning outcomes would have been somewhat different.

So, the teacher needs to bear in mind that the dramatic context provides an appropriate lens through which children can examine the theme.

'Could you say more about choice of context?'

Perhaps this is a good time to return to our key examples which we first introduced and examined in Chapter 3 when we talked about choice of learning area or theme.

What we will do now, in each key example, is identify the contexts the teachers selected and give reasons for their choices.

Key Example 1 – 6/7-year-olds

Theme/Learning Area	*Context*
taking plant species from an environment and the consequences of this for local people	Ministry of Agriculture expedition to rainforest

Reasons for choice of context
Remember that the teacher is deciding on the particular fictional circumstances which will be created by the drama to explore the theme. Remember, also, that we

have stressed the human dimension in choice of theme. Since an action is already implicit in the theme – that is the act of removing a species of plant from its environment – in identifying the context, it only remains to settle on the particular circumstances which will be created in the drama to enable that 'removal' to take place and for the consequences of that action to be revealed for the purposes of the drama. A range of possibilities come to mind – the vandalising of the flower-beds in the local park; deforestation by international logging companies; over-harvesting of crops; 'slash and burn' agriculture; the smuggling of rare orchids, for example. However, in the end, the teacher here chose the collecting expedition by botanists to the rainforest as the context.

The inspiration for this was drawn from the fact that while natural sources for new medicines are still being discovered in plants, the relentless assault upon the world's rainforests means that with every species lost the potential for another cure is also lost. But, the context for this complex and serious situation has to be pitched at a level six-and seven-year-olds can understand.

On a dramatic level, this context also provided the imperative for generating a range of thought, feeling and action on the part of the pupils which would address the various learning goals that the teacher had in mind when beginning to plan the drama – see Chapter 3 as a reminder.

Key Example 2 – 8/9-year-olds

Theme/Learning Area	*Context*
emigration – what makes human beings give up what they know and take a long and difficult journey in the hope of something better at the end?	Victorian London as gold find in Australia is announced

Reasons for choice of context

As you will remember from the discussion in Chapter 3 about how the teacher chose this particular theme, the children in this class almost all came from families who had undertaken such journeys as these. Some of the children, themselves, had journeyed from other places and others had parents or grandparents who had relocated. Some had come to this part of London from other towns and cities in England, but most of their families originated in places such as Bangladesh, Hong Kong, India, Ireland, Nigeria, Pakistan, the Philippines, Scotland, Somalia, Turkey and the West Indies.

This choice of theme, therefore, was highly relevant to this group of children, but it was important not to select a context which by featuring one real life journey would, by definition, exclude and devalue the journeys of the others. Therefore, finding a context which was removed in time and was an analogy for the sorts of journeys undertaken by their families was very important. By locating the drama in a journey that none of their families had really taken but which paralleled the experiences of them all, meant that they all could be involved equally in the fictional journey *and yet* draw upon their family histories as fuel for the drama.

Key Example 3 – 11/13-year-olds

Theme/Learning Area	*Context*
creation theory versus evolution theory–why does a tension exist between those who hold different views about the origins of life on earth?	present day Jamaican law firm preparing to defend a client

Reasons for choice of context

The brief given to the teacher in this instance, as outlined in Chapter 3, was very wide-ranging. The pupils involved were highly capable and in need of a challenge. The controversy implicit in the theme selected already had a strong theatrical precedent in the play *Inherit the Wind*. But these were Jamaican children and the teacher was not sure that the pupils involved would be particularly interested in exploring the finer, historical details of the 1925 'Scopes Monkey Trial' in Tennessee when rationalists challenged the law forbidding the teaching of evolution theory – the inspiration for the stage-drama. However, the *issues* raised by the historical events could still have a continuing resonance for the pupils.

Sustaining interest in a court drama over the five-day period of the workshop was both unlikely and undesirable. Also what was needed was a dramatic context in which the pupils could be engaged in meaningful tasks. So, it was *preparing to defend a case* that was similar to, but not identical with the original that, in the teacher's view, provided the most appropriate context in this particular situation.

What can be drawn from the three key examples in relation to the choice of dramatic context? We can see that all of the teachers were concerned with *balance*. They each needed to find a context in which the various requirements of the curriculum learning area, the social and personal learning, the learning about drama itself and the needs and interests of the children could be held in balance and *facilitated* by the process drama structure.

'But, doesn't narrowing down to the specific dramatic context mean that teachers may omit things from the curriculum brief?'

It is unrealistic to expect any particular learning experience to provide children with *all* there is for them to know about the subject matter. What is important is allowing the children to engage with the particular circumstances of a social encounter so that they will come to their own understanding about the learning. So, even where a theme appears to have been already narrowed down to what seems to be little more than a minor incident, the potential it holds for unpacking the curriculum is huge.

The Dolly Johnson Story is a case in point. This incident refers to the first woman, a laundress in Kingston, Jamaica, to have contracted cholera in the serious outbreak in the 1840s. She is mentioned in the autobiography of Mary Seacole and it is believed that she contracted the disease by taking a basket of laundry from an infected ship which came to Kingston from New Orleans. The incident, however, has great potential for learning within it and may be explored through drama in several different dramatic contexts.

Dolly Johnson Story

Place	Time period	Event
Dolly Johnson's Laundry	1840s	the quarantining of the laundry
Jamaica National Assembly	1840s	taking steps to control the cholera outbreak
on board the infected ship	1840s	dispatching laundry ashore
on a film set	modern times	making a film of The Dolly Johnson Story
at an archaeological site	modern times	excavating the laundry buildings
at a new hospital	modern times	commissioning a new ward named after Dolly Johnson

So, within the relatively narrow confines of The Dolly Johnson Story (narrower say than 'the transmission of infectious diseases' or 'the history of Public Health') it is still possible for the teacher to find a range of dramatic contexts in which to actively explore the theme. Sometimes, a teacher may be surprised at finding the 'universal' in the 'particular'. For example, a deeper understanding of public health issues in general, as well as those of Jamaica in the 1840s, may be gained as a result of engaging in some shape or form with Dolly Johnson's personal tragedy.

Identifying the right context or spending time carefully selecting a context pays dividends because it may serve to personalise big issues and so serve to make familiar the unfamiliar.

summary, in preparing a dramatic context for process drama it is important
:member that all drama is essentially about people and their relationships,
,cerns, hopes, fears, aspirations, celebrations and rites of passage. So, the teacher
v..1ose theme is *well-chosen*, will have used this understanding to inform her
choice. With this understanding, it is possible, therefore, for that choice to be
stimulated by reference to such diverse areas as history, geography, sociological
events, current affairs, literature, science, personal relationships, visual and
performing arts, political events, the contents of specific school curricula, myths,
legends, cultural forms, moral issues.

The spectrum of human experience is the content source for process drama and
it is from this that you will make your choice of theme or learning area. This done,
you will then make your choice of dramatic context and in doing so, you will be
aware that a small and particular set of circumstances holds within it the possibility
of exploring the big issue.

'Where to now?'

Well, having decided on what the pupils are going to learn about and the fictional
circumstances in which it is to happen, you now need to decide on the people who
will inhabit the fiction. In other words, you are now faced with selecting the roles
that both the pupils and you will play in the drama. And this choice is the subject
of the next chapter.

CHAPTER 5

Role

Key Question:
'Who are the pupils and the teacher going to be in the drama?'

Let's begin with the children. We have pointed out that one of the cornerstones of process drama is the innate predisposition of children to take on imagined roles and place themselves in imagined circumstances in order to understand the world in which they live. Indeed, the fundamental activity in any theatre genre is taking a role – that is, imagining that you are someone else in a fictional context and exploring a situation through that person's eyes.

It is obvious, therefore, that when the teacher sets about planning a process drama experience for her class, she needs to understand that she will be setting up a situation in which the children will be behaving as if they were people other than themselves. It is also clear that she needs to ensure that the roles she plans for the children will 'match' with both the learning area and with the dramatic context in which it is to be explored.

The choice of roles for the children might seem a big task. However, it's not quite as difficult as it sounds. As soon as the teacher has identified the dramatic context in which she wishes to explore the theme or learning area the roles which are required for the drama will, actually, begin to suggest themselves.

For example, if we look at one of the examples from Chapter 4, The Vikings, there is a very clear relationship between the context and the roles in the drama. The roles, in fact, begin to emerge quite naturally from within and round about the dramatic context.

Place	Time period	Event	Roles
Holy Island	Viking times	the Viking landing	*Anglo-Saxon monks on Holy Island*
mainland village	Viking times	preparing to repel the invaders	*Anglo-Saxon villagers*
monastery	Mediaeval times	chronicling Viking invasion	*Mediaeval monks*
village	modern times	commemorating defence of village	*modern day village community committee*
film studio	modern times	making a film about the invasion	*film production company*
archaeological site	modern times	excavating site of battle	*archaeologists*
museum	modern times	setting up living museum display	*curators*

You will find that as soon as you start to think about the context in which the theme can be explored then possible roles for the children will pop up into your mind by association.

The second set of examples from Chapter 4, on Water Conservation, show a similar pattern of development.

Place	Time period	Event	Roles
plant nursery	present day	finding ways to reduce water costs	*horticulturalists/ gardeners*
hospital	present day	devising systems for recycling waste water	*hospital staff*

mountain forest	present day	preventing lowland flooding created by deforestation	*forest rangers/ environmentalists*
desert oasis	present day	calculating water needed to get caravan across the desert	*camel drivers and desert traders*
village community	present day	designing ways of storing water for use in dry season	*farmers*
life raft after plane crash at sea	present day	deciding how to collect potable water to stay alive	*survivors*
polluted river	present day	experimentation with natural means to decontaminate water such as water hyacinths	*biotechnologists*

In looking at these examples, we hope that you can see that the roles are mainly groups of people associated with the chosen dramatic context. They are groups of people whom one might reasonably expect to find intimately involved with these particular situations and circumstances.

When identifying roles for your pupils, this group aspect is important for a number of reasons. The first is that you will want to ensure the full participation in the drama by everyone in the class. In the examples given above, this would be fairly straightforward since we have Anglo-Saxon villagers, film makers, monks, forest rangers and even biotechnologists – all groups large enough to accommodate a class of pupils, however large; an important consideration when class sizes can vary so enormously.

These examples present themselves to the planner quite readily, as is most usually the case. There can be occasions, however, when you have to think a little bit more carefully in order to identify an appropriate grouping. This is often the case where the stimulus for the drama is a story or literary text.

Some stories may, indeed, provide lots of opportunities for group roles, *The Pied Piper*, for example. Rat catchers, townsfolk, the children of Hamelin spring immediately to mind and all could provide very satisfactory roles through which the children could engage with the learning. But, in say, *The Three Little Pigs*, the teacher may have to think more widely around the immediate story so that group roles can be identified and the whole class accommodated. It would not be very enabling of the drama nor the children's learning to have endless sets of three little pigs! However, if we choose a dramatic context such as one in which the Wolf is put on trial, then we may reasonably invite a group of witnesses to come forward and give evidence for or against him. In this way we can ensure the participation of the whole class of children.

While this is clearly an example from the early years, the same principle applies when working with older pupils. In a process drama approach to *Romeo and Juliet*, for example, members of the class might assume the group role of the Montague Clan speculating on the origins of 'the ancient grudge' between themselves and the Capulets. In turn, they might well assume the group role of the Capulets in order to explore the grounds on which they would forbid Juliet ever to marry a Montague.

This identification of a group role, which will embrace all of the pupils, is a key task for the teacher planning process drama not least of all because it helps to focus all of the class on the issues and tasks of the drama. In addition, the group approach assists in achieving consensus as well as in the application of a common point of tension to the drama, both key issues in successful process drama and both of which we will return to in further detail in subsequent chapters.

'Do you mean that all the children are expected to play the same kind of part in the drama?'

In the sense that they will all be villagers, or monks or Capulets, this may seem true, *on the face of it*. However, within the group identities we have mentioned, there lies enormous scope for individual differences, levels of participation and opinions. This is not only desirable, but essential to the success of the process drama.

Let's look at the examples of contexts through which to examine how the Anglo-Saxons responded to the Viking invasion. In each context, the group roles we have identified all have scope for individual difference. If we look closely at the Mediaeval monastery example, we see that the group role is that of monks who are engaged in writing chronicles. This provides the drama with a framework in which all the class can work together. However, there is still scope for a variety of occupations within the overall context of chronicling, for example, scribe, paper maker, quill maker, ink maker, illuminator, librarian, woodcarver, leather worker, weaver, bookbinder and so on. These will enrich the drama and provide opportunity for the action, reaction and interaction we mentioned in Chapter 1, while still maintaining the community perspective and the group focus of the drama which is the chronicling of the Anglo-Saxon response to the Viking invasions.

'Could you go over this again, please?'

Perhaps it would be a good idea at this point, to reintroduce our key examples of initial planning for process drama. This time adding the roles we used to begin the dramas.

Key Example 1 – 6/7-year-olds

Theme/Learning Area	*Context*	*Pupils' roles*
taking plant species from an environment impacts negatively on the local people	Ministry of Agriculture expedition to rainforest	botanists

As we discussed in the chapters on Theme and Context, this drama set out to examine some of the effects upon indigenous peoples of the exploitation by others of their native plant species. Having settled upon the context of a Ministry of Agriculture expedition to locate and collect specimens of a recently identified plant, the teacher was then faced with the choice of roles for the children.

In fact, a number of different roles suggested themselves – people of the rainforest, ministry officials, scientists, doctors, expedition organisers – all of these groups of people could have a legitimate presence within the context of this drama which offer the children a gateway into the desired learning. However, ultimately, the teacher selected the role of botanists for the children.

'Can you say why?'

To begin with, botanists form a group which would naturally engage with the substance of the drama, that is to say, with plants and their habitats. Botanists work 'in the field' regularly and so it is reasonable to suppose in the fiction of the drama that botanists could go on a plant collecting expedition to the rainforest. Working in a scientific way is also implicit in this role, as is a level of expertise. These are all attributes which have embedded in them the possibility for action and this is important because one way of describing drama is as *ideas in action*. Such action allows the teacher to enable the children to both explore some of the ways in which drama allows the ideas to be made manifest *and* allows the children to engage with the curriculum. In other words, through the actions which are implicit in the roles, the teacher has the means by which to engage the children in both of the strands of learning we discussed in Chapter 1 - Strand A about drama and Strand B through drama about other things.

Key Example 2 – 8/9-year-olds

Theme/Learning Area	*Context*	*Pupils' roles*
emigration – what makes human beings give up what they know and take a long and difficult journey in the hope of something better at the end?	Victorian London as gold find in Australia is announced	inhabitants of London

In our second running example, we can see that although the theme and context of this drama were very different from the previous one, the planning challenge faced by the teacher remained the same. That is, she needed to find roles for the children which would bind them together as a group of people. She also needed to ensure that this would be a group who could reasonably be expected to be in the chosen context. This grouping, as inhabitants of London, is not so tightly defined by occupation as the botanist example. However, this drama did not require this. The nature of the theme and context meant that this drama was not concerned about 'professional activity' but about examining an aspect of the human condition. It was therefore important for the teacher to choose a group role for the pupils which would provide a community in which there was a range of values, perspectives and attitudes but a collective interest in the finding of gold in Australia.

Key Example 3 – 11/13-year-olds

Theme/Learning Area	*Context*	*Pupil's roles*
creation theory versus evolution theory – why does a tension exist between those who hold different views about the origins of life on earth?	present day Jamaican law firm preparing to defend a client	junior lawyers

As we saw in Chapter 4, this drama already had a strongly theatrical precedent in the treatment given to the events of the famous 'Scopes Monkey Trial' in the play, *Inherit the Wind* (as well as its subsequent film versions). So the drama being planned was immediately working with potentially controversial material, and a legal context *suggested by*, but *not* recreating the historical events of the original trial in 1925. However, an enormous range of possibilities still existed for developing roles even within that narrowed context. Because of the real context within which the drama took place, the teacher needed to ensure that the roles selected for the children would provide a framework in which the issue could be addressed in a cool and balanced manner. Therefore, the roles of lawyers, with the attendant demands of that profession to consider *evidence* rather than being swayed by a tide of emotion, was made by the teacher. Further, a defence rather than a prosecution brief was considered more desirable socially, as well as being more conducive to the gathering and careful weighing of supporting evidence. The pupils' junior position in the law firm served to bind them together because they could be reasonably expected to do most of the leg-work in evidence-gathering, an important consideration for this task-based drama.

'What do you mean by binding?'

In process drama, we all need to be 'in the same boat', so to speak, yet must hold a very individual perspective on our common situation. So, selecting roles for the pupils which bind them together from the outset of the drama, is *critical*.

The roles the pupils assume in the drama may immediately bind them together in different ways. For example:

- *by kinship* – family members, members of a tribe, descendants of common ancestors
- *by occupation or skill* – printers, shoemakers, needle workers, vets, sail makers, pharmacologists
- *by belief or ideology* – monks, nuns, vegetarians, politicians, pilgrims to Mecca, Rome or the Ganges
- *by knowledge* – guides, language translators, navigators, stockbrokers, alchemists
- *by induction* – baptismal candidates, deputies, awardees, members of a Hall of Fame, members of a secret society
- *by age* – teenagers, pensioners, centenarians, juvenile offenders
- *by qualification* – graduates, driving instructors, licensed food handlers, first aiders, paramedics
- *by uniform* – soldiers, nurses, police officers, traffic wardens, astronauts, Salvation Army
- *by need* – homeless people, orphans, alcoholics, famine victims
- *by location* – air passengers, prisoners, hospital patients, palace guards, villagers
- *by common experiences* – mothers, widows, home owners, war veterans, refugees
- *by interest and hobby* – collectors, train spotters, dog fanciers, golfers, flower arrangers.

So, if we look again at our three key examples, we can see that in the Rainforest drama, the pupils were in the role of botanists, bound together by *skill and knowledge;* in the Gold Strike drama, they were in the role of Londoners, bound together by *location;* and in the Creation/Evolution drama they were bound together by *qualification and occupation.*

Of course, the above list is by no means exhaustive and many other elements can bind people together. Indeed, it may be possible to classify a role under several headings. For example, soldiers might be bound together simultaneously by occupation, ideology, uniform, location and common experience. The main point, here, is that looking at ways in which people are bound together like this can help you as a teacher identify roles which quickly bring a sense of cohesiveness to the drama. However, the selection the teacher ultimately makes will always need to be the one which best serves the learning area within the chosen dramatic context.

'But won't the group role restrict the chance for the pupils to express themselves, individually?'

Of course, as we said in the opening chapter, drama is a powerful means of enabling personal expression. However, this needs to be fostered within a framework which is disciplined and structured but not strictured. It is also essential to remember that drama is a *collective, social* art form which is created by participants working collaboratively. Random self-expression, therefore, by a class-sized group of individuals will rarely facilitate the development of the drama.

Not unreasonably, then, drama in schools frequently had a bad press in the days when the main justification for pursuing it as an educational activity was that it would foster self-expression in the child. Mass self-expression all over the school hall was often perceived as chaos – and often this was the correct perception! Fortunately, thinking and understanding about how and what makes drama so effective as a learning medium has moved on as the discipline has grown and developed.

Having to focus the class on the task at hand regardless of the subject or discipline area, be it science, history, literature or whatever, is part of basic classroom management whatever approach (whole-class, small group or individual seat work) is being taken. So, what the drama teacher is attempting to ensure in planning for process drama is that in order to negotiate her way through a potential minefield of individual attitudes, opinions and emotional responses to the situation under scrutiny she first of all establishes a group focus on the theme through a group identity within the fiction.

There are, of course, other dramatic genres which are part of the drama within education canon, which *do* encourage and, indeed, demand that children work individually – when examining monologue, for example, or working on the development of non-verbal means of expression. However, these *usually* fall outside the parameters of process drama in which it is the cohesiveness of the group as it moves through the experience of the drama together, albeit with shades of response, which is essential.

'Is it possible for the pupils to be themselves in a drama?'

This can *appear* to happen quite frequently in process drama, though, most often, it would be misleading to say that the pupils are being themselves. They must undergo some change in behaviour once they accept the fictional context of the drama. Since process drama is a genre of theatre in which the participants' engagement with the role is not so much deepened by characterisation as by attitude, then it is often the attributes they bring to the drama which are of uppermost concern.

Often, when the role is not clearly defined in a *situated* identity (i.e. occupation, social position), the pupils may simply be 'good at finding things out' or 'good at helping'. A good example of this was a one-session drama with a class of nine- to ten-year-olds, exploring the theme of Latitude and Longitude. The children appeared to be themselves in the first part of the drama, enjoying themselves at the beach, playing with a ball. However, the teacher and children had agreed beforehand that there would be, hidden in a tree trunk, an old piece of paper containing the clue to some buried treasure. This clue contained the latitude and longitude coordinates but only the teacher knew this.

The main test for the children in the drama was how far they could build the tension by *not* finding the paper. The point of this was to get everybody focused on the clue, indeed, playing with dramatic irony, so that the longer they took in not finding it, the more its presence in the room grew and the more important it would be when it was eventually 'discovered'. The pleasure the children had in keeping themselves and the teacher in suspense was enormous, too. The point we are making here is that, although to an outside glance, this looked as though the children were merely themselves, in actuality, by virtue of the suspension of their disbelief, they had entered a fiction and were *in role* as themselves.

Let's take another example. One memorable session on Power and Authority was conducted with a class of 18-year-olds and 20 visiting (real) soldiers. In the drama, the pupils took on the situated roles of police officers and other uniformed personnel, while, dressed in fatigues, the soldiers played themselves by acting out how different their own behaviour might be when they were out of uniform – in other words, soldiers in uniform, in role as themselves out of uniform. The point of this was that the soldiers felt the military uniform affected their own bearing and deportment as well as other people's perception of them. They noticed how people, particularly uniformed police officers, adjusted their behaviour towards them according to whether the soldiers were in or out of uniform.

Sometimes in a drama, the situated identity of the role, is not anything like as clear as monk, Anglo-Saxon villager or biotechnologist. In a drama about a lost child, a class of eight-year-olds, simply became people who had offered to go out and look for him but, once into the drama, they very quickly began to assume *adult* attitudes and responsibilities and create for themselves previous 'experience' on which to draw during the search.

Almost always in their own dramatic playing, children take on adult roles. This is very readily understood. Children are extremely perceptive and early in life recognise that the power to control and change the status quo lies firmly in the hands of adults. Having recognised this, they assume adult roles in their dramatic playing in order to understand and empower themselves. As teachers, therefore, it should come as no surprise to us that, when we come to create process drama with children in school, that they will naturally assume adults' roles in the drama. In our earlier examples from Chapter 4, on the Vikings, unless the teacher specifically makes it otherwise, then the drama will *not* be about Anglo-Saxon village *children* or *child* novices at the monastery because pupils will, almost certainly, naturally assume that the drama is about adults.

This understanding is very important for the teacher when planning process drama. Recognising that pupils readily take on adult roles will impact on her choice of roles and, indeed, dramatic context.

However, one of the differences between process drama and other genres of theatre within education, lies in the nature of the teacher's active involvement with the unfolding drama. In process drama, the teacher frequently needs to take a role in the drama *herself.* This is known as teacher-in-role or TIR, for short, and in this aspect of planning, you also have to plan your role in the drama as well as the children's.

'Could you explain more about teacher-in-role?'

One of the cornerstones of process drama, mentioned earlier, is a recognition that learners who gain a sense of ownership about their learning by having the opportunity to help shape its direction, have a greater commitment to it and gain more from it as a result.

In a sense, this implies that there needs to be a more even-handed partnership between the teacher and the pupils than is sometimes the case in the classroom. As we pointed out a moment ago, children are very astute in understanding social power structures and this is one of the reasons they take on adult roles in their own dramatic playing, as a means of empowering themselves. This is another part of the foundation upon which process drama rests and we actively build upon this to help construct the drama.

However, this understanding that children have about 'how things work' can also work against them becoming involved in shaping the drama and, therefore, developing their sense of ownership about it, unless we are careful in our planning. As teachers, how many times have we all felt that the children we are working with are giving us the answers that they think we want, *because* we are the teachers and they are in the more subordinate position of pupils?

Clearly there are times when this situation is both necessary and desirable. But, there are times when it will not do, and one of those times is when we are wanting to work in the process drama genre.

We are certainly *not* encouraging any abrogation of responsibility on the part of the teacher. Teachers will always carry the ultimate responsibility for what goes on in their classrooms. However, within the process drama framework that we are setting out in this book, which is absolutely predicated upon teachers making informed, professional decisions about learning within a curriculum structure, we are suggesting that the usual relationship between teacher and pupils needs to be set to one side, *at times*, as one means by which children can gain a sense of ownership about what they are doing.

One of the most effective ways of managing this power shift, within the context of the drama, is through teacher-in-role.

'But I can't do that, I'm not a good actor!'

This is an understandable reaction but there are two things to bear in mind which will make the prospect of teacher-in-role less daunting than it seems. Firstly, teacher-in-role is not actually about acting in the external sense of putting on a costume and finding a voice and set of mannerisms for a character. But, it is concerned with enabling pupils to enter the drama. Secondly, if we think about it for a moment, we will recognise that teaching can be a performance art in itself, anyway. We give performances in our classrooms, daily. As soon as we stand in front of the class we are, in effect, 'commanding our stage'; by the way we modify the way we speak, our facial expressions and body language, we 'deliver our dialogue'; when we respond to the behaviour of the children we are teaching we may give the response that the 'script' demands which may not be the response we would otherwise give – how many times have we all wanted to laugh but have felt the need to be stern? – we often withhold what we know, in order to create an effect. Under these circumstances we are playing the part of a teacher – we are acting the role.

For example, a teacher, observed in a class of rising five-year-olds in Jamaica, was teaching a mathematics lesson – her learning focus being the numeral '4'. After proceeding through a whole range of traditional reinforcement activities including songs (4 green bottles, 4 men went to mow), I-spy games (4 fruits, 4 animals, etc.)

and actions (draw a number 4 with your finger – one stroke down, one stroke across, another stroke down) she suddenly did something quite different. She turned to the chalkboard and then, turning slowly around to the children with a terribly worried expression on her face, she said, anxiously, 'Oh, dear! I've forgotten how to make a 4!' The children needed no further prompting since they understood immediately from her expression, that the teacher was inviting them to 'play' and was inviting a response which they duly gave – that is they explained to her the method of making a 4 which she had just taught them (one stoke down, one stroke across, another stoke down). The teacher then proceeded to make life very difficult for her young charges by assuming the role of a most inept pupil. However carefully the children instructed her, she managed somehow (trying to make the 4 on the chalkboard) to get it all wrong. She pushed the children to the absolute limit of their patience before she finally managed to get it right. A young student teacher, who had been observing this class was heard to remark, 'She's in role' which, of course, the teacher was. She was clearly demonstrating a type of behaviour totally at odds with her accepted teacher persona and well outside the normal expectation of her young pupils. This teacher was very deliberately teaching from a position of ignorance. She was clearly portraying herself as a total incompetent, displaying a type of behaviour which effectively shifted the power structure within the classroom. The teacher had voluntarily yielded her power to the children so that they could become 'the teachers' and she 'the taught'. So, it was not only her role which had shifted. By taking on the role of the incompetent she had, by inference, negotiated new roles for the children (i.e. teachers) which they were more than happy to accept.

This is an example of a teacher confidently stepping into a role and deliberately denying her own knowledge in order to empower the children with knowledge and allow them to have 'the upper hand' in the learning situation. We are sure that you will be able to recall numerous situations in which you have employed a similar teaching strategy.

You will recognise that there was never any indication that, because the teacher had abrogated her power, she would lose control of the class. The children clearly understood the nature of the 'playing' structure at work in this instance and were happy to 'play by the rules' and to relinquish their new-found power in order for the next phase of the lesson to be introduced. What lingered in the classroom after this encounter was a sense of what Dorothy Heathcote has referred to as 'colleagueness'. It is not a sense of the teacher imposing her curriculum on the children so much as the development of a partnership between teacher and pupils as they move through an experience of mutual discovery. The children never lost sight of the fact that they were operating within a fictional context and the teacher never lost control of her class.

If you have ever created a similar type of situation in your classroom, and we are certain that you will have done, then you are ready to take what is a small step into teacher-in-role within a process drama.

Here is an example in which a deliberate process drama was created. In the real context of a nursery class of three-and four-year-olds in London, the children who stayed all day took a nap after lunch. It was the practice of the school for the children to remove their outer clothing before going to sleep. Unfortunately, this particular class of children were not very competent at dressing themselves again afterwards and staff found themselves spending an inordinately long time in helping children to put their clothes on. So the teacher decided to find a means to help the children to become more adept in this skill.

She told her class that she had a 'friend', Sue, who was having some difficulty. The friend hoped that, as she had heard from their teacher, they were particularly kind and helpful children, they might try to help her sort out her problem. The children readily agreed to meet the 'Sue' – the teacher-in-role.

The teacher slipped around the corner and returned in a sorry state. She was very upset and hesitant about approaching the children. The children were bemused by 'Sue's' appearance and started to giggle. The teacher-in-role was then able to point out that this was the very problem that she had. She told them that ever since she had left home that morning people had been laughing at her and she didn't know why. She thought this was very rude and unkind and couldn't think what she could possibly have done to make people behave in that way.

In fact, the teacher had dressed herself in a completely higgledy-piggledy fashion. She had gloves on her feet, shoes on her hands, her cardigan on back to front and a handbag slung around her neck. No wonder the children laughed.

However, as the sincerity of her role came across, the children's attitude rapidly changed and they became very caring of her. Very gently one little girl took the teacher's hand, patted it and told 'Sue' that she had got her clothes on wrongly and that this was why people had been laughing at her. 'Sue' asked how this could be rectified and of course the children responded that she should dress herself properly. Now came 'Sue's' confession that she didn't know how to and the tentative request that the children explain what to do.

The interchange that then followed, rather like the example of the number 4, saw the teacher-in-role make things difficult. They became more and more exasperated as 'Sue' failed again and again to do her buttons up, but at the same time, ever more precise in their instructions until, at last, 'Sue' was ready to face the world properly turned out. With this accomplished, 'Sue' said a huge thankyou to the class and, with a parting request for them to say hello to her friend, their teacher, she slipped round the corner again.

The teacher then returned to her class in her own clothes, no longer in role to be greeted with a chorus of 'Your friend, Sue, was here and she said to say hello! She had all her clothes on back to front and we helped her to get dressed properly. She was upset by people laughing but we made it all right'.

There are two important points here. Firstly, the children behaved in a completely responsible fashion during the meeting with 'Sue', were *all* focused on the problem and did not run rampage though the teacher had apparently relinquished her authority. Secondly, even though the children knew perfectly well that 'Sue' was their teacher pretending to be someone else, their ready suspension of disbelief and their obvious innate understanding of how drama works, meant that when the teacher returned the children were bursting to tell her all about the meeting with 'Sue' and what they had done to help her and to absolutely slip back into the usual teacher–pupil relationship when this drama was over.

The point we are making here is that if you take on a role in a process drama and by doing so 'stop being teacher' for a while, this does not mean that you will not be able to regain your previous relationship with your class. Remember that children are used to coming in and out of role all the time in their dramatic playing. They recognise that, when one of them takes on the role of 'king' and gives orders which the rest willingly carry out during a pretend game, after it is over the relationship between the 'king' and his 'subjects' reverts to the normal, peer friendship. Similarly, they will recognise that when their teacher comes out of role, the normal classroom relationships apply once more, just as was the case when 'Sue' had left the nursery.

'So is teacher-in-role only for use with young children?'

No. We do not see the use of TIR as being restricted to use with young children. We have just used these very simple examples from the early years as a way of indicating the roots of the strategy in normal teaching behaviour.

This next example is of another one-lesson drama, this time with a class of 16-year-olds. The teacher is consciously using a TIR approach but in a situation where both pupils and teacher still play roles very close to their own, situated identities in the school so the fictional circumstances of the drama are not too far removed from the school experience familiar to both of them.

The teacher introduced the session by explaining to the pupils that she was going to use a TIR approach. They agreed that when the teacher moved from behind the desk she would emerge in role. She had not indicated what her role would be but she carried in her hand a letter and almost immediately began to negotiate her fictional role; that of principal or head teacher. This fact was laid in through what she said to the pupils and, of course, she also had to make sure that they clearly understood who they were in the drama, too. 'Good morning, student council members!' she said. 'Is this the full number of people on the student council?' 'Nobody is missing?' So, immediately the pupils knew who they were in the drama; no longer themselves as pupils but members of the student council. The teacher continued by apologising for the short notice of the meeting, commended everyone for attending before revealing her own role in the drama. 'As principal of this school, I have always tried...'. So now they knew who she was and, of course, the letter was important to the drama because it, purportedly, contained an expression of concern from the student council about the rate of teenage pregnancy in the school and a request for the installation of a condom vending machine in the senior school toilets. When asked whether anyone knew about this letter, it was hardly surprising that no one among the pupils responded. However, when further pressed, one or two entered into the drama by acknowledging their part in sending the letter and began openly to voice their concern. Very quickly more of the pupils became more willing to enter the action more fully and began to consider the pros and cons of the condom vending machine as a solution to the problem.

At all times, the contribution of the 'principal' was slow, measured, considered, authoritative (not authoritarian) as various opinions were aired. After a very lively discussion, the teacher signalled that she was coming out of her role as principal and informed the class that the drama would now move on. Re-entering her role in the drama as principal, she then refocused the roles of the pupils so that they very quickly understood that they were now parents at a PTA meeting. When the contents of the letter from the student council were revealed to the pupils in role as parents, it was like a bombshell. Many of them expressed vehement opposition to the proposed vending machine. The final result was that, after a long period of deliberation, the pupils, in role as parents, embarked upon the introduction of a mentoring programme and the development of a timetable of structured extra-curricular activities, as well as additional intervention strategies for needy students of the fictitious school.

We have chosen these three examples because they are very simple and help to illustrate how the shift from the real context into a fictional one can be achieved by only a small shift in the context and the behaviour of the teacher.

'In the examples you've given, the teacher still has the power, doesn't she?'

When planning TIR, the teacher has to remind herself what the 'accepted' power structure in classrooms already is. Implicitly, the teacher is endowed with the power. Her status, relative to that of the pupils, is high and can be perceived as a barrier to the realisation of the more open, creative learning relationship between pupils and teacher which is needed in a process drama. At its worst, this implicit relationship produces authoritarian teachers, resentful pupils and sometimes open and direct confrontation between the two. Yet shifting the power structure in classrooms is something that can, and frequently does, happen naturally and almost subconsciously.

'Isn't this a bit manipulative?'

Well, smoothly effecting shifts in the relative status of the participants in process drama is critical. The implicit power structure of the classroom we referred to above, with the teacher's status high relative to that of the pupils, will be open to change within the fictional circumstances of the drama. One power structure belongs to the real life context of the classroom while the dramatic context clearly opens up an opportunity for a renegotiation of the participants' relative status. A teacher-in-role need not always take up an authority position within the drama. This was clearly illustrated in our example with the teacher and the numeral 4. She appeared to give up all her power when she admitted, in role, that she couldn't remember how to make a 4. But the teacher's status within the drama has more to do with 'voice' than social position. For example, if the teacher was to take on the role of a king we might be forgiven for assuming that she had taken on a high status role in order to provide some modicum of insurance for her real life role of teacher. However, although a king may be quite obviously of high social standing he can still be in low status relative to those around him if he is uncertain, needs advice or has a terrible problem or dilemma facing him. Alan Bennett's highly successful stageplay, *The Madness of George III*, clearly plays with just such a situation so that the main action hinges on the vulnerability of the monarch relative to those around him. On the other hand, a tramp or other personage of low social standing may assume high status if his manners are impeccable relative to those around him and if he demands high standards of etiquette and good manners in others.

'Why is an understanding of role status so important for the teacher?'

In earlier chapters we noted that learners who have a sense of ownership about their learning have a greater sense of commitment to it and gain more from it as a result. The task of all teachers, surely, is to maximise the possibilities for pupils to learn. If we accept this, then process drama, particularly with teacher-in-role as a central strategy, is a powerful means by which teachers can enable this to happen. Because the usual hierarchy of the classroom is set to one side within process drama, the way is open for the children to make a contribution to the shape and direction of their own learning. The teacher sidesteps her usual position of ultimate authority, final arbiter of situations and fountainhead of knowledge – especially when she chooses a role which is more vulnerable – so that the children are confronted with the decision-making, researching, problem-solving and team working necessary to resolve the central dilemma of the drama.

Having established this background from which process drama, with teacher-in-role, springs so readily, we now need to return to our three key examples to see how the teachers in these situations introduced TIR into their planning and to consider the reasons which led them to the choices they made.

Key Example 1 – 6/7-year-olds

Theme/Learning Area	Context	Pupils' roles	Teacher's role
taking plant species from an environment impacts negatively on the local people	Ministry of Agriculture expedition to rainforest	botanists	civil servant from the ministry

Reasons for choice of teacher's role

So, the teacher had decided on the role of botanists for the children. Having done this, a range of possible roles for herself in the drama had to be considered. She could, for example, have taken on the role of fellow botanist, Chief Scientist, Minister of Agriculture, one of the indigenous people of the rainforest, civil servant from the Ministry of Agriculture. All of these roles could have enabled her to enter the drama. However, any choice in planning process drama has consequences for the drama, that the teacher will need to bear in mind. In this instance, the teacher needed to think through the effect each of these possible roles might have on how the drama might unfold and select the one which would most suit the needs of the children and the needs of the drama. Each one carried a particular body of knowledge, level of expertise, authority and responsibility. The task for the teacher was, again, one of balance. She needed to select the role which would most adeptly facilitate the children's learning by most adeptly facilitating the drama. The advantages offered by the civil servant role were several. Firstly, by becoming an administrative assistant to the absent Department Head, she put herself into the position of being able to mediate between the 'botanists' and the 'boss'. By declining to take on the role of the boss, she maintained a level of authority by virtue of being his right-hand person but relinquished ultimate authority because she was not him. From this position, she was able to throw the pupils back on their own resources, decision-making processes and such because she did not have the ultimate say and, furthermore, the person who could have had it, was absent. This choice of role had further advantages. By becoming an *administrator* rather than another botanist, she ensured that she did not have the expertise, within the fiction of the drama, to which the pupils could defer. In fact, she created the reverse situation by the choice, so that she, from her position of ignorance, could probe, challenge, enquire, speculate, query and support the pupils in their role as the experts and, therefore, in their learning by empowering them, and, *in some respects*, disempowering herself.

Let's look at Key Example 2, where the teacher did something similar but through an apparently much less flexible choice of role.

Key Example 2 – 8/9-year-olds

Theme/Learning Area	*Context*	*Pupils' roles*	*Teacher's role*
what makes human beings give up what they know and take a long and difficult journey in the hope of something better at the end?	Victorian London as gold find in Australia is announced	inhabitants of London	ship's captain

Reasons for choice of teacher's role

In this example, we can see that there was a greater 'distance' between the roles of the pupils and the role that the teacher had selected for herself. In the first example, in which the roles were bound by skill and knowledge, the teacher, although not in role as a botanist, herself, chose a role which was attenuated to the same field by virtue of the tasks incumbent upon a civil servant in the Ministry of Agriculture given responsibility for facilitating the expedition. However, here, in Key Example 2, the pupils are in role as inhabitants of London, bound together by location, but the teacher's role represents the possibility of *going somewhere else*. Although she could have taken on many others' roles in the drama, fellow Londoner; returnee from Australia; public official, the Beadle for example; map maker; the choice of ship's captain provided her with the best opportunity to give information in role about the gold strike in Australia – by virtue of 'having just returned' *and* the means within the drama, the ship, for the Londoners to go to Australia to seek their fortunes. She mitigated against the authority of her role, as the drama unfolded, by revealing that she needed the Londoners to help crew the vessel in order that she, and they, could sail for Australia.

Key Example 3 – 11/13-year-olds

Theme/Learning Area	*Context*	*Pupils' roles*	*Teacher's role*
creation theory versus evolution theory – why does a tension exist between those who hold different views about the origins of life on earth?	present day Jamaican law firm gathering evidence for a case	lawyers	head of law chambers

Reasons for the choice of teacher's role

Having made the decision to cast pupils in the roles of 'lawyers' because of the need to gather evidence, it might seem rather obvious that an authority role like 'Head of Law Chambers' should have been chosen by the teacher in order for her to enter the drama. Yet several others were available to her but were eventually discarded, including defendant, office cleaner, fellow lawyer, newspaper reporter, presiding judge, for example.

Head of Law Chambers might, then, not be quite such an obvious choice, particularly if, as we have been implying, the teacher was supposed to be trying to give up some of her power. However, roles of authority figures like 'the boss' do not always have to be what they seem. In this particular instance the interests of the Head of the Law Chambers were clearly aligned with those of her staff. What was clearly binding them together was the common ground of their profession. The Head of Chambers' strength may well have resided in her ability to 'lead' the defence of a client, but she remained, nonetheless, heavily dependent upon her colleagues' ability to furnish her with a body of evidence without which she would be unable to argue the case in court.

We hope that we have made clear here that teacher-in-role is fundamental to process drama and not simply a strategy in the sense of being one among many theatre forms available to the teacher. For us, *TIR enables the teacher to operate strategically from within the drama and so negotiate and renegotiate circumstances within the fiction in order to enhance learning opportunities.*

Once the teacher has identified the theme, the particular dramatic circumstances in which it will be explored, and who she and the pupils are going to be in the drama, she is still faced with the enormous question – what are we actually going to do in the drama. There has to be some element present which galvanises us into action. The prerequisite for this call to meaningful action we call 'Frame' and that is the subject of our next chapter.

CHAPTER 6

Frame

Key Question:
'How will the roles be framed? That is, which viewpoint will the roles have in order to create tension in the drama and how distanced do the roles need to be?'

Let's begin this chapter by returning for a moment to the key examples we have been carrying through since Chapter 3. So far, for each of them, we have identified theme, context, pupils' role and teacher's role, as follows:

Key Example 1 – 6/7-year-olds

Theme/Learning Area	*Context*	*Pupils' roles*	*Teacher's role*
taking plant species from an environment impacts negatively on the local people	present day briefing at the Ministry of Agriculture	botanists	civil servant from the ministry

Key Example 2 – 8/9-year-olds

Theme/Learning Area	*Context*	*Pupils' roles*	*Teacher's role*
what makes human beings give up what they know and take a long and difficult journey in the hope of something better at the end?	Victorian London as gold find in Australia is announced	inhabitants of London	ship's captain

Key Example 3 – 11/13-year-olds

Theme/Learning Area	*Context*	*Pupils' roles*	*Teacher's role*
creation theory versus evolution theory – why does a tension exist between those who hold different views about the origins of life on earth?	present day Jamaican law firm gathering evidence for a case	lawyers	head of law chambers

For each one of these examples, we know the theme – that is, what it is we want the children to learn about; we know the context – that is, the particular fictional circumstances in which the drama will unfold; and we know the roles – that is, who the pupils and teacher will be in the drama. But, in each of these examples, the critical element is missing – that is, the *imperative for active participation*. We don't yet know what it is that will drive the participants to action in the drama. What is missing is *dramatic tension*.

'Why is dramatic tension so important?'

We pointed out early in this book that in process drama the participants – the children and teacher together – 'write' a play as the narrative of the drama unfolds in time and space and through action, reaction and interaction. We need to realise, therefore, that the elements of theatre which work in *all* well-crafted plays also need to be invoked in process drama. One of those crucial elements is dramatic tension.

Dramatic tension is the fuel which fires the imperative for action in a play. It is created by the friction which exists at the interface between the differing, and sometimes rival, values, beliefs and aspirations of characters. As the drama unfolds, the reactions and responses of the characters are motivated by their own, often competing, attitudes to the turn of events and the behaviour of others.

The key factor which impacts upon the creation of dramatic tension in a process drama is that there is no predetermined, written script into which the playwright will have already woven the motivations for characters' responses and actions.

During the rehearsals for the staging of a play, actors will frequently ask, 'What's my motivation?' and seek the answer from the subtext of the playscript so that their performances will be informed by an understanding of what makes their characters 'tick'. In process drama, participants need to understand this too, but cannot draw the answer from a script. This is, actually, critical. Just giving children a role in a process drama is quite sterile, both in terms of learning about and through drama, without the imperative for active participation that is provided when the inclusion of dramatic tension throws the circumstances and the events of the drama and the relationships between the roles into sharp relief.

Therefore, the teacher needs to provide it for them by other means and the means to the creation of dramatic tension in process drama is called 'frame'.

'Why call it frame?'

Frame is a concept refined by the eminent Canadian sociologist, Erving Goffman, whose work in *Frame Analysis* was adapted and applied by Dorothy Heathcote to process drama. Goffman uses 'frame' to refer, essentially, to the *viewpoint* individuals will have about their circumstances and which helps them to *make sense of* an event or situation and to assess its likely impact upon themselves as individuals. Translated into terms of process drama as a genre of theatre, we could say that Goffman's frame constitutes a means of laying in the dramatic tension by situating the participants in relation to the unfolding action.

'This seems a bit complicated'

Well, yes, it is rather, but we consider that 'frame' is the most important process drama planning principle of all. Getting this one right really does go a long way to ensuring that the drama you create with the pupils will be of high quality and, therefore, offer the greatest learning opportunity. So, it's worth spending some time teasing out the key issues surrounding the concept of frame. It might seem a bit complex at first but by the end of this chapter we are confident that you will have the knowledge and understanding to ensure that the roles in your drama are well-framed.

'Why is it so important for the roles to be framed?'

Well, we can say that in real life, whenever we come upon a set of circumstances we do not come to them neutrally. We see them from our own particular *point of view* – a window which has been shaped by our previous life experiences. While these points of view are unique to ourselves in their minute detail, nonetheless, groups of people who have experiences or interests in common often have similar viewpoints. For example, when there is an occurrence within the world of education, those of us who are teachers will see it from a particular viewpoint which is different from those who are not teachers. While this does not imply that we will all have the *same opinion* about it, it does mean that we will share a *collective concern* by reason of what binds us together as a profession and the effects which a likely outcome of that occurrence will have upon us.

In planning process drama, we need to ensure that we lay in for the participants, a collective concern for how the events of the drama will unfold because it is in these events, and the roles' responses to them, that the learning is located. In the Chapter 4 discussion of pupils' roles, we argued for the need to find ways of binding groups together. This, in fact, is the first step on the way to creating the collective concern. So, in our key examples, the botanists, the Londoners and the lawyers are already connected to the learning area by reason of their common interest, that is by who and what they are.

However, there is a further step to take. We should not allow ourselves to think that, just because we have laid in the common interest, we have also provided dramatic tension. At this point, we have only succeeded in preparing a state in which the *possibility for dramatic tension* to be created lies. We now need to find a mechanism through which we can shift the position of the roles from one of merely a common interest, born out of a group identity, into the desired *collective concern*. This shift is achieved by the addition of *investment*. On the surface, common interest and collective concern may seem to be interchangeable terms, but they're not. In providing a 'real' need to engage ever more deeply with the events of the drama (and therefore the learning) we ensure that the roles *care* about what has happened, is happening and might happen and are motivated into action. This, now, provides the collective concern. And with the collective concern comes dramatic tension because while collective concern endows all the participants with an investment in the outcome of the drama they will *not* all necessarily want the *same* outcome.

If we return to what we were saying earlier about dramatic tension being born from the friction between differing and often opposing attitudes, values and aspirations of characters in a play, then we can see that this friction is precisely what the frame provides. However, frame can actually do this in three ways.

- Firstly, through the differences in opinion between the pupils' roles – 'I think we should negotiate with the strangers', 'No, I think we should run', 'I think there may be something in this for me'.
- Secondly, through the differences between the pupils' roles and the teacher-in-role – 'You'll all have to work overtime and for less money', 'But my family can't survive on what you pay now'.
- Thirdly, through the differences between the collective view of the pupils and the teacher-in-role, together, and an absent antagonist – 'What are we going to do to get past the monster?'

Whichever of these ways the teacher plans to use frame to invoke dramatic tension, it will lead to greater focus and commitment to resolving the 'dilemma' of the drama and, consequently, a greater potential for learning. This is because frame enables, further, the contextualisation of learning and promotes the pupils' opportunity to take ownership of their learning and help shape its direction.

'How does frame help this pupil ownership of learning to come about?'

Well, we would argue that drama, as much of life, is concerned with the exploration of what binds people together; the inborn instinct to relate to others in both positive and negative ways so that these bindings become the seeds of *talk and action*. Moreover, they become the seeds of the *type* of talk and action demanded by the drama – botanists' talk, travellers' talk, lawyers' talk, and what it is they are actually doing – gathering evidence, collecting plant species, or travelling across the world to make their fortunes.

If we accept that drama is essentially an art form which has talk as its currency, then it is clear that we must ensure that this collective concern is *present in the drama* at the outset. The importance of this is that it propels the participants into discourse – *it will mean they have something to say* because they have a 'handle' on the situation.

Of course, people communicate not only by the words they choose but also by the non-verbal signals of body language which combine with the words to make the meaning plain.

Moreover, there are times in most genres of theatre when non-verbal means of expression are forefronted – mime and dance spring obviously to mind. In addition, we do not wish to imply that the verbal nature of drama means that the characters in a play all converse happily together. Indeed, there are times when characters in plays clearly do not do so, just as in life. Often, drama is as much about the conflict of people not communicating with each other as it is about the reverse. Nonetheless, ultimately, we do wish the pupils in process drama to use the spoken language to negotiate the meaning of their unfolding play and, through it, the learning inherent within the drama.

Through our own practice we have come to the conclusion that the quality of the process drama experience and, therefore, the quality of the learning it generates, most importantly rests upon the teacher's ability to provide the most appropriate role *and frame* for the learners. In effect, frame is the means to the creation of dramatic tension and, as we hope we are making clear, in order to get good learning you need good drama and to get good drama you need good dramatic tension!

In genres of theatre which require performers to take on roles within a play with a pre-written text, it is quite clear that those characters have no previous life experience which will shape their viewpoint on the events of the play. Until the actors lift the text from the page and bring the characters to life, they have only ever been a series of words on paper. However, if the playwright has done the job well, the subtext of the play and the in-built dramatic tension will give the actor his role's point of view. This will mean he will know what motivates the role and will enable him to approach the unfolding events within the play with an attitude which will drive his performance.

In the process drama genre, too, the roles that the children will take on quite clearly do not have previous life experience. They are, actually, in an even less developed state than roles in a play text because process drama does not have a predetermined written script. Coupled with this is the fact that the people who are going to create the roles – the children – have, themselves, a more limited range of life experiences on which to draw.

'So how can the pupils proceed?'

It should be clear from what we have said so far, that this function of frame refers to the way in which it empowers children in the communication process within the drama. Basically, it gives them something to say by providing what Dorothy Heathcote calls a 'power stance' – in other words, a position of sufficient *authority* from which to proceed in the drama. The importance of empowering them in this way demands that the choice of the *communication frame* is considered carefully. We do not wish to leave the children floundering in the drama.

But there is something of a paradox here. It is the job of teachers to enable children to come to understand the world around them in order that they can function more successfully within it. This means that we are constantly seeking to enable children to go from the known to the unknown so that they meet new ideas, concepts and understandings or are enabled to gain new insights and shifts in perceptions about things they know already.

Drama is a powerful process by which these ends can be gained but it does imply that we are regularly establishing dramas about times, places, peoples and circumstances which are beyond the experiences of our pupils. In fact, this means that what we regularly are asking them to do demands that they step onto the shaky ground of the unknown. In drama terms this usually means asking them to take on the roles and behave as if they are people of whom they have little prior knowledge, and herein lies a potential for floundering.

'How can the teacher guard against this?'

Well, we need to ensure that the children have *one* foot on firm ground and we can do this by selecting a communication frame which will enable them to draw on their own real life experience so that they can bring authenticity to the drama. Let's look at some examples of dramas to make this clearer.

In a drama set in the west of the United States, it's not a matter of being cowhands but cowhands *who have lost their horses;* in a drama set in the West Indies of the early 1800s, it's not a matter of slaves but slaves who are *secretly planning a rebellion,* or in a drama set at an archaeological site, it's not a matter of archaeologists but archaeologists *who must complete the dig within a week.* The important factor in all of these examples is that they are not merely descriptive but function dynamically. What is important is not what the people look like or where they are, so much as what they feel and think; that is, *what drives them.*

In these examples, pupils who cannot know the experience of cowhands *do* know something of loss and therefore it is on that level they enter the drama and so can immediately talk with authority about dealing with the problem of the lost horses. They will enter the drama, not with the experience of enslavement but they *will* have an understanding of secrecy. Nor will they have archaeological experience but *will* have great understanding of the constraints of time.

If we return to our key examples, in Key Example 1 we can see that the teacher's planning ensured that the roles of the pupils were not just botanists but they were botanists *who had to keep their expedition secret.*

Key Example 1 – 6/7-year-olds

Theme/Learning Area	Context	Pupils' roles	Frame
taking plant species from an environment impacts negatively on the local people	present day briefing at the Ministry of Agriculture	botanists who ... *Teacher's role* civil servant from the ministry	must keep their expedition to the rainforest secret

In Key Example 2, the pupils were not merely people living in London in the early 1850s but were people living in London *who were discontent with their lives.*

Key Example 2 – 8/9-year-olds

Theme/Learning Area	Context	Pupils' roles	Frame
what makes human beings give up what they know and take a long and difficult journey in the hope of something better at the end?	Victorian London as gold find in Australia is announced	inhabitants of London who... *Teacher's role* ship's captain	are discontent with their lives in London

In Key Example 3, the pupils were not just in role as junior lawyers but as junior lawyers *who needed to meet a deadline for gathering and presenting evidence.*

Key Example 3 – 11/13-year-olds

Theme/Learning Area	*Context*	*Pupils' roles*	*Frame*
creation theory versus	present day	lawyers who...	need to meet a
evolution theory–why	Jamaican		deadline to
does a tension exist	law firm	*Teacher's role*	present evidence
between those who hold	gathering	head of law	for the official
different views about the	evidence	chambers	hearing
origins of life on earth?	for a case		

From this, we hope that it is clear that in each of the key examples, the pupils had a point of view – an attitude about the situation – and were sufficiently empowered to enter into dialogue in role.

'Is there anything else I need to know about frame?'

Well, in the second part of the key question at the beginning of this chapter, we also mentioned the need for roles to be *distanced.* This equally important function of frame, working in tandem with the communication/tension function, protects children into the experience of the drama through *'distancing'.*

This really is an important issue, so let's spend some time examining it.

If we accept that it is the teacher's intention to take children into new areas of experience, often these will be so far removed from their everyday lives or so sensitive that they will need to be approached with care. We have mentioned already the importance of selecting a communication frame which will still allow the pupils to have one foot on the firm ground of their own experience but we must also consider the *distance* function of frame as a means of protecting the participants into the drama experience. Often, in practice, this means that it is better to approach the core of the drama from a tangent, rather than diving into the middle of something in a way which leads the pupils, because they have not been given the circumstances under which to do anything else, to engage at a superficial or disruptive level, resulting in the quality of the drama and, therefore, the learning being undermined.

In other words, taking a 'cooler' approach to the learning area is often better than taking a 'hot' one.

'How does distancing relate to context and role and to the theme/learning area?'

Distancing is possible *both through time and emotional relationship* to the main area of exploration. We want to make this essential feature more explicit so we have represented it diagrammatically.

The grid model (Figure 6.1), sets out in detail the critical planning concepts of learning area, context, role and the two functions of frame in relation to a theme/learning area which is both far removed from the experiences of the pupils and potentially harrowing. As we have tried to show in this range of approaches, it

The Two Aspects of Frame
Theme/Learning Area: The First World War

W.W. B

Learning Area	Context	Role	Frame	
			Communication	Distance
The horror of warfare techniques	In the trenches in France	Soldiers...	who have no gas masks	**HOT** None
The physical/mental consequences of war	In a field hospital	Nursing/ ambulance personnel...	who are understaffed and under-equipped	Not by time, a little by relationship
The strategy of war	In strategic command HQ	Generals/ military staff...	who cannot afford further defeat	Not by time, a little by relationship
Consequence for those left behind	At the town hall waiting for new casualty lists	Family members...	who have heard of new losses	Not by time, a little by relationship
The propaganda of war	Film studio/ location	Film makers...	who are instructed by government to make post war documentary with a positive spin	Somewhat by time, more by relationship
Importance of Remembrance	The Cenotaph	Veterans...	who are late for ceremony	Not by relationship but by time
Cultural significance of war	Museum	Curators...	who cannot display all items	By relationship and by time
Symbolic representation of war, the role of women	Design studio	Sculptors...	whose design has been rejected for not including women's role	Greatest distance by time and by relationship **COOL**

Figure 6.1

is possible to engage with the material in numerous ways – not all of which are included here by any means. What the grid illustrates is a range of possible roles to be taken by the children, the contexts in which the drama might unfold and the essential frames which provide the dramatic tension. We have moved through varying degrees of both time and emotional distance from the main area of exploration, indicating a shift from what we have earlier described as a 'hot' experience towards a 'cooler' one.

'Could you explain the grid in a little more detail?'

Well, let's take two of the examples from the grid and expand them to reveal how the lessons might progress. By doing this we hope to show the relationship between the two aspects of frame working together with role and context to maximise the quality of the drama experience for the children.

If we look at the 'hottest' situation in terms of the distance function of frame, in which the pupils take on the roles of soldiers, we can see that there is a potential for the kind of disruptive behaviour or superficial engagement which we referred to earlier. In this situation, the pupils are not distanced by time at all so there remains a real possibility for inappropriate behaviour because what the pupils are likely to know about soldiers is fighting! However, by careful selection of a communication/tension frame, namely as soldiers *who have no gas masks*, we are able to minimise this possibility. We are able to cool down the situation considerably because, now, the action of the drama will be focused on deciding how to cope with the gas mask situation and *not* with hand to hand combat. The pupils will be able to draw upon their real life experiences of 'making do' and problem-solving, so creating a better chance of them engaging with the learning area of the drama in a manner which is more meaningful and less superficial.

Now, let's look at the 'coolest' example on the grid, which involves the pupils in role as sculptors. This is the coolest situation because the participants are distanced greatly by *both* time and emotional relationship, so already the communication and distance functions of frame reduce the potential for disruption, though not necessarily for superficiality! But, in addition, the careful selection of the communication function of frame offers the potential for shifts in perceptions about the war with regard to gender.

The whole grid shows different roles placed in dramatic contexts which have communication and distancing frames at incrementally greater removes from the hot zone of the fighting. Each example addresses the same broad learning area of The First World War. But, because the roles, context and frame differ in each individual example, the learning outcomes will be different. However, it needs to be emphasised that although each leads to a particular aspect of the area of learning, none is 'better' that any other. Each does, however, offer a different learning experience. The skill of the teacher is to make an appropriate choice dependent upon the particular class with whom she is working. This will be governed by the age, experience, social health, curriculum concerns and so on, of the class.

'Could you show how frame fits into the key examples?'

Of course, now would be a good time to look at them again and add this next layer to the planning.

Key Example 1 – 6/7-year-olds

Theme/Learning Area	Context	Pupils' roles	Frame
taking plant species from an environment impacts negatively on the local people	present day briefing at the Ministry of Agriculture	botanists who ... *Teacher's role* civil servant from the ministry	must keep their expedition to the rainforest secret

Reasons for choice of frame

These six- and seven-year-olds had no experience of being botanists and little experience of the technical language of botany. However, all children of this age understand what it means to keep a secret. Therefore, at the outset of the drama, they were able to engage authentically with the experience as the group discussed the arrangements to be made which would ensure the covert nature of the expedition was not compromised. Moreover, being botanists rather than rainforest dwellers gave the pupils a cool perspective sufficiently distanced from the hot zone to be able to examine the learning focus of the 'threat to the environment' objectively while still being engaged by the excitement of going on an adventure which pupils of this age so enjoy.

Key Example 2 – 8/9-year-olds

Theme/Learning Area	Context	Pupils' roles	Frame
what makes human beings give up what they know and take a long and difficult journey in the hope of something better at the end?	Victorian London as gold find in Australia is announced	inhabitants of London who... *Teacher's role* ship's captain	are discontent with their lives in London

Reasons for choice of frame

Given that this drama took place within an historical context, the children quite clearly could have no experience of being Victorian Londoners. However, they all had experience of being 'fed up' and wishing that things could be different. This is, after all, a feeling which we all understand. They could, therefore, quickly enter the drama by articulating why they were feeling discontented with their lives. You will notice that in this example, there is little distance from the hot zone. However, we must remember that this learning area was not beyond the experience of this particular class of children. The overwhelming majority came from families which had relocated to London from a range of places, both intra- and inter-national.

Key Example 3 – 11/13-year-olds

Theme/Learning Area	*Context*	*Pupils' roles*	*Frame*
creation theory versus evolution theory–why doesa tension exist between those who hold different views about the origins of life on earth?	present day Jamaican law firm gathering evidence for a case	lawyers who... *Teacher's role* head of law chambers	need to meet a deadline to present evidence for the official hearing

Reasons for choice of frame

Clearly, this class of pupils did not have experience of being lawyers; however, they all understood very well the pressures of time. Moreover, they understood the principle of responsibility to other people, in this case, the client and the Head of Chambers who needed the evidence on time. The pupils were distanced by means of delaying the advent of the hearing so that the drama focused on the assemblage of evidence rather than an emotive confrontation in the courtroom.

It is worth remembering that, in each of these examples, the teacher drew upon her knowledge of the pupils in her class to help her select a frame which was appropriate for *them*.

So, in this chapter we hope that we've made clear that whenever you choose a frame, the communication function (offering collective concern and power stance and therefore an *affective engagement* with the drama) together with the distancing function (which protects into the experience) combine to offer the greatest potential for high quality drama and, therefore, learning.

'Is the planning complete now?'

There are still two further aspects of planning we need to bring into the equation before the teacher is ready to begin the drama. One is *'strategies'* and we will come back to this later. The other aspect is *'sign'* and that is the subject of the next chapter.

CHAPTER 7

Sign

Key Question:
'What artefacts, personal items, sounds, images and so on will I need to bring significance to the events of the drama?'

People make sense of the world around them by a continuous processing of information. This information may be presented in many different forms, for example, the written or spoken word, pictures, diagrams, photographs, maps, road signs, clothing, architecture, furnishings, works of art (drama, dance, music and visual art); in fact, the list is endless. These potentially information-bearing phenomena are known as 'signs' and the academic study of signs and how meaning is communicated in society is known as 'semiotics'.

'How is this relevant for process drama?'

There's no need here to go into too much detail about the discipline of semiotics, but effective planning for process drama requires some insight and understanding about the ways in which signs may be generated and interpreted. It might be helpful if we begin by considering how signs are used by theatre practitioners to create meaning for an audience.

In the theatre, objects, light, sound and words are organised for significance. A performance in the theatre is a highly selective, deliberate event which is designed to enable the making of meaning for its audience. In other words, all that the members of the audience see and hear has been deliberately selected in order to clearly communicate the meaning of the play to them, but they must *read* it.

In effect, theatre is a semiotic system which is concerned with processes of signification and communication via which meanings are generated and exchanged. Each individual sign-carrying element is known as a 'sign-vehicle'. Together, they combine in order to communicate information to an audience.

'This seems complicated'

Looking at some specific examples might clarify this. If the stage is set with a dining table on which there are four place settings the audience is being led to believe that there is a reasonable expectation that four people will arrive to eat a meal. If only three arrive the audience may further reasonably conclude that someone is missing. Further clues may be yielded by (a) what the three actors say to each other, (b) their gender, (c) their age, (d) their costume – including the colour and/or style, (e) the decor of the room, (f) sound effects, (g) lighting, and so on. This totality will be read and so lead the audience to recognise a crofter's cottage, a hotel dining room or a king's palace.

However, in the theatre there is yet another, perhaps even more important, aspect to sign. Sign-vehicles may be invested with special features, qualities and attributes that they do not have in real life. While in real life the utilitarian function of an object is usually more important than its signification, in the theatre it is the signification which usually takes precedence. Furthermore, this signification can be divided into two categories. Firstly, the sign-vehicle may stand for something which is concrete and secondly, it may stand for something which is abstract. For example, a stick, when functioning in the concrete mode, can represent a range of objects including a golf club, a spear, a donkey, even a baby or a dance partner. In the abstract mode it can represent the wand of truth, the rod of correction, the sword of justice.

In summary, the theatrical sign is polyfunctional. In other words, theatre gives permission to things to be read as things other than they are. A long piece of cloth can function as the train of a dress, an ocean, a river, a wall, a tent or mountains when used in the concrete mode or a confused state of mind, security, a feeling of claustrophobia or imprisonment, if tightly bound, when used in the abstract mode.

It will be clear that an appreciation and understanding of this principle of the polyfunctionality of the theatrical sign is also critical for the successful planning of process drama experiences. However, we don't need to create a full-blown theatrical setting for process drama to take place. In fact, it would be counter-productive to do so. What the teacher needs to do is to use things such as artefacts and personal items – documents, images, sounds and three-dimensional objects for instance – to direct the children's attention and help them to explore actively the precise focus of the lesson. What we actually need to do is *combine the children's willing suspension of disbelief; a well-chosen context; roles and frame, with the teacher's careful selection of a few well-chosen signs, which the teacher has prepared in advance, and which will hook the children into the focus of the drama at its outset.*

It might be useful at this point to introduce a somewhat pared down version of the American semiotician C.S. Pierce's classification of signs, namely *symbol, icon* and *index* (Figure 7.1).

Pierce's Sign Classification

Symbol	Icon	Index
signifies as	signifies by	signifies through
a replica which	means of	an existential
must be interpreted	resemblance	relationship

Figure 7.1

'Why is this classification useful for process drama?'

If, as we have already stated, in the theatre objects, light, sound and words are organised for significance, it might be useful to learn a little more about the nature of those signs. After all, the more we understand things, the more likely we are to use them to best advantage.

A *symbol* signifies as a replica which must be interpreted – for example a crown is not only something to be worn on the head but also may represent the institution of the monarchy itself. Symbols of this nature are used extensively in the theatre as in life. Flags representing nations, colours representing political affiliations or emotional states or social conventions – stereotypically the widow wears black, the virgin wears white, the harlot wears red. In addition, because of the polyfunctionality of the theatrical sign as identified by Erika Fisher-Lichte, a chair can stand for a motor car, a mountain, a stepladder, an umbrella, etc.

An *icon* signifies by means of resemblance. A good example from the theatre might be a portrait or scenery where a pictorial or graphic representation of a person, object or setting is used.

An *index* signifies through an existential relationship. For example, a knock at the door points to someone on the other side, a telephone ringing points to someone wishing to speak, smoke points to the possible existence of a fire. So, 'symbol' may correspond to both metaphor and metonym, 'icon' to the more literal and representational, while 'index' is about relatedness.

In her pioneering drama work, Dorothy Heathcote eventually grew to understand that, in an educational situation, the semiotic system operating in the theatre would need to be adjusted to the requirements of education . However, her approach developed more along the lines of Jerome Bruner's classification of 'symbolic, iconic and enactive representation' than of the Pierce trichotomy (Figure 7.2).

Bruner/Heathcote's Trichotomy		
Symbolic	**Iconic**	**Expressive**
relating to the linguistic or numerical function	relating to the visual or graphic function	relating to the active, performing function

Figure 7.2

At the risk of paraphrasing Bruner, much of what happens in schools occurs in the symbolic domain, principally where letters, words and numbers are the things that stand for concepts, objects and calculations. In most educational systems worldwide, it is this system of the symbolic representation which is privileged. Pupil competence is measured in terms of how well they can handle these writing and numerical systems.

Iconic representation appears to be less privileged in education, so that art, craft, technical drawing, modelling and draughtsmanship are often regarded as vocational studies and are therefore less valued than academic subjects. Finally, there is enactive or expressive representation – voice, body, dance, drama, music, and these tend to be valued least of all in education yet, ironically, are highly prized in terms of the position they hold in high culture – theatre, opera, ballet, for example.

Once the drama teacher begins to understand that she has symbolic, iconic and expressive systems of representation at her disposal she can begin to fulfil the requirements of the drama more efficiently by plugging in to the most appropriate signing system. Because drama is perceived primarily as an expressive art form, teachers are frequently, mistakenly as it happens, tempted to move their work directly into the expressive mode. Just as the director of a play must consider many other aspects of staging apart from the expressive aspects of the performance – for example, sets, costumes, sound effects – so the teacher must sign into the classroom the elements of the drama in the most appropriate way. An example may help.

Good signing in process drama eases the need to have somebody keep the drama going because good signing will generate tasks which will further generate new signs and tensions. An example of this at work was during one of the first drama experiences we had with Dorothy Heathcote which was with residents of an adult facility in the North East of England for people with mental disabilities. Trying to get some (expressive) horses, played by members of the drama team, back to their owner, we had to take them on a journey. Part of that journey took us on a train journey through a long dark tunnel containing horrors of our own invention. Everyone was protected into the experience because we were imagining those things which would frighten the horses but, of course, we were working through our own basic fears as well, by drawing insects, spiders, snakes and ghosts on a long roll of paper representing (iconically) the inside of the tunnel. Knowing that we were framed as people who had to protect these horses, we were then freed to realise new tensions by creating the most horrible things imaginable but with which we felt we could cope. The very act of drawing them somehow disarmed them of their potential to frighten us, while they retained their horrifying potential to scare the horses.

'But why is this so important?'

This identification of symbolic, iconic and expressive systems of representation is not merely an interesting piece of educational theory but constitutes a very useful tool which has the potential to assist teachers enormously in identifying the ways in which signs will be generated in process drama. This is, after all, a genre of theatre in which some signs will be prepared in advance, while others will have to be generated as they are required. The precise nature of these signs will have important consequences, too. What we have said already, and are trying to emphasise, is that because they are doing drama many teachers feel bound to gravitate directly towards the expressive system of representation. But this is not always the most desirable option. Perhaps another example will help.

Two teachers, team teaching a lesson on decision-making with a class of 45 seven-year-olds, opted to use the dramatic context of a restaurant and it is interesting to see exactly how the different systems of representation we have been outlining were used during the course of the lesson.

One of the teachers, out of role, spoke with the children and explained that they were going to be part of a drama about a restaurant. The teacher then gave out circles cut from old computer paper which she explained were going to be their plates. She then asked them to decorate the edges, the borders of the plates, with their crayons. While they were getting on with that task, the teacher turned to the chalkboard and wrote the words 'Minnie's Restaurant – Menu', followed by a list of dishes available. The children were then invited to make their choice from the menu and to draw their dinners on their plates. Only very gradually, through the talk of the teacher, the eventual appearance of the menu on the board and the children's careful decoration of the plates and drawing of their dinners, was the sense of 'restaurantness' signed into the classroom.

In other genres of theatre, many of the elements which would go into signing the idea of restaurant might have been constructed, painted and preset before the start of the play, for example, menu, tables, chairs, place settings. And, indeed, the teacher here, could have prepared many of those things in advance. She chose instead to get the children to make them as part of the learning activity and up to this point all their activities were clearly located within the symbolic (writing the restaurant name and menu) and iconic (decorating and drawing on the plates) systems of representation.

This approach also helped the teacher to build up the idea of the children's roles as customers in the restaurant before she finally put on an apron and picked up a notebook and pencil to sign her role as waitress and they entered fully into the expressive events of the drama with her question to them, 'Would you like anything to drink with your meal?' Teachers can benefit from knowing that there are alternative ways of doing things as a result of the availability of these systems of representation. If the requirements of the drama call for the idea of a dog in, say, a drama about the police canine division, how will the dog be signed into the room? Knowing what you do about these systems of symbolic, iconic and expressive representation, you now have a choice. You can sign the idea of a dog, symbolically, by writing its name or the word 'dog' on a piece of paper, sticking it on the wall and negotiating with the pupils that, in the drama, this is where the dog is chained. You can sign the idea of a dog, iconically, by making a drawing or three-dimensional model of the dog in its kennel. Alternatively, you could create the dog expressively but in this case you run the risk that somebody may end up barking uncontrollably because someone will be 'playing the part' of the dog.

In their work on *Bo Peep*, Nigel Toye and Francis Prendiville avoided the barking dog through a series of controlled signs. Francis, in the role of the farmer, wore a tweed cap, carried a shepherd's crook and set down on the ground a brightly coloured dog bowl before whistling for the dog and calling its name. When the nursery pupils with whom they were working were invited to come forward one at a time to pat the dog, they were able to locate the (invisible) dog, because they knew where the dog's bowl was, and so could enter into the drama.

The system of signing chosen will determine not only how effectively something is signed into the room but will also determine what you can do with it. That is, the nature of the engagement.

When a teacher conducted a drama about a distressed farmer whose cow, Daisy, had fallen down a big hole, the six-year-old pupils, in the role of farm workers, were faced with the enormous problem of getting Daisy out of the hole. What considerations went into signing Daisy for the pupils? The symbolic representation of Daisy's name written on a piece of paper would sign her presence adequately, but would not serve the enactment of the rescue very well. Iconic representation would be fine, that is having Daisy represented by a large drawing of a cow (a life size three-dimensional model would have been both too literal as well as impractical), but hauling a drawing of Daisy out of the hole as part of the rescue just wouldn't ring true for anyone either. Having someone representing Daisy expressively, might have meant having someone in a cow mask, mooing incessantly, which in all probability would only have shattered the intense and urgent manner in which they devised their ingenious rescue apparatus and carried out their plan. Actually, in order for Daisy to be rescued she had not to be physically represented at all.

This sounds paradoxical but, ironically, by not having a visible cow, the pupils were liberated to 'see' her through the eyes of their imagination. They were able to imagine the level of her distress, the awkward way in which she was stuck in the hole, the amount of space they had to work in and the size and weight of the animal which had to be rescued. The plan they devised for the rescue involved the construction and use of lifting apparatus operated by everyone pulling together on ropes, while Daisy was soothed by tempting her with her favourite food and the sounds of familiar voices. This apparatus was also created in the imagination of children so that it was possible for them to 'feel' the weight of Daisy on the lifting platform and know they had a big job to do. So, the teacher was faced with finding a different means by which to sign Daisy's presence which did not rely upon something concrete. In fact, this was achieved through expressively signing the hole by having the children stand around its perimeter and signing Daisy symbolically through the children keeping her calm by singing their choice of song, 'Daisy, Daisy'. Daisy had to be present in the drama but invisible for the purposes of the rescue.

So, what the teacher uses as signs, as well as how they are used, will vary from one drama to another. However, there is one principle in their selection which remains constant for *all* dramas. That is the need for the chosen signs to be clear, uncluttered and absolutely focused on the learning area of the drama, since it is the children's learning which is critical.

'You mentioned earlier that some signs will be prepared in advance. Can you say why?'

As we've said before, process drama has many things in common with other areas of the curriculum in respect of the planning and preparation the teacher needs to undertake before the lesson begins. You will be very familiar with the need to prepare your teaching materials in advance for many of the lessons you teach in other areas of the curriculum. In a nutshell, signs which are prepared in advance can be regarded as your teaching materials for the lesson. Some may be concerned with helping to transform your working space, some will be used to evoke a mood, some to foreshadow events of the unfolding drama, some to create absent others (that is to say, represent someone who is not actually present), some to identify community, some to identify role and/or status; all will need to lead the pupil's attention to the focus of the drama – the learning area or theme.

For example, in a drama about life in a fishing village, the teacher needed to indicate that fish stocks had been seriously depleted by over-fishing and undesirable fishing practices such as the use of dynamite. This had reduced the boats to taking immature fish as the larger fish had gone. The teacher's choice of sign was governed by the need to focus the attention of the pupils on the learning area. Therefore, she finally selected a real fishing net but in addition the pupils in role drew small fishes on pieces of paper which were then placed in the net. What is important here is that the teacher needed to restrict the size of the fish in order to evoke the dilemma, which she achieved by limiting the size of the paper which the children had been given. This may seem rather obvious but is actually crucial. She could not have rejected what the children had created but if the fish had been too big then the sign would have worked against the theme of the drama rather than supporting it.

So, what we have here is an example of sign helping to establish the context of the drama both through what the teacher has prepared in advance – the fishing net – and by the sign generated by the pupils in role – the fish.

'Can you relate this to the key examples?'

Well, let's return to the key examples again, and see which signs the teacher prepared.

Key Example 1 – 6/7-year-olds

Theme/ Learning Area	*Context*	*Pupils' roles*	*Frame*	*Sign*
taking plant species from an environment impacts negatively on the local people	present day briefing at the Ministry of Agriculture	botanists who… *Teacher's role* civil servant from the ministry	must keep their expedition to the rainforest secret	photograph, of rare plant, secrecy pact, writing materials, clipboard, requisition slips

Reasons for choice of signs

In this drama the teacher needed to find a sign to focus the pupils' attention on the plant which was to be the object of the botanists' expedition to the rainforest. Ultimately, she selected a photograph of a real plant. Firstly, this choice was made because it was photograph of an unusual plant (in fact a species of orchid) with which the pupils were unfamiliar. However, the teacher also chose this photograph because the plant was placed against a black background which gave no point of reference to the size of the plant. This was important. It meant that the pupils were at liberty in the drama to 'discover' specimens and no matter what the size they reported, they would all be right. In role, both teacher and pupils were able to conclude in the expedition's log that 'it starts as a small plant but can grow to immense proportions'. In order to support the frame of the drama, the teacher also created a 'confidentiality agreement', to which the botanists had to add their signatures, and Ministry requisition slips and other bureaucratic impedimenta.

Key Example 2 – 8/9-year-olds

Theme/ Learning Area	Context	Pupils' roles	Frame	Sign
what makes human beings give up what they know and take a long and difficult journey in the hope of something better at the end?	Victorian London as gold find in Australia is announced	inhabitants of London who… *Teacher's role* ship's captain	are discontent with their lives in London	broadsheet announcing gold strike and a public meeting, large wall map of route between England and Australia, small map of Australia, gold nugget

Reasons for choice of signs

Here, the teacher created a broadsheet flyer which announced both the finding of gold in Australia and a public meeting for people who wished to take passage to Australia. This sign worked to focus the pupils on the learning area by the use of counterpoint. While the teacher could have used any number of artefacts to suggest a discontented life in London, she actually chose to create a sign which would place that discontentment into high relief by holding out the tantalising prospect of a means for things to be different – going to Australia and making one's fortune – so fuelling the action of the drama. She reinforced this with the presence of a nugget of gold while, at the same time, symbolising the enormity of the undertaking by the presence of a huge map of the route between the two countries which actually extended around two walls of the classroom.

Key Example 3 – 11/13-year-olds

Theme/ Learning Area	*Context*	*Pupils' roles*	*Frame*	*Sign*
creation theory versus evolution theory–why does a tension exist between those who hold different views about the origins of life on earth?	present day Jamaican law firm gathering evidence for a case	lawyers who... *Teacher's Role* head of law chambers	need to meet a deadline to present evidence for the official hearing	brief from client, law books, documents, file

Reasons for choice of signs

In this example, the teacher had to communicate clearly the nature of the law profession which was achieved through the presence of the law books. These, along with the files and other documentation, also helped to point the pupils in the direction of the research with which they were to be engaged throughout the week of their activity. However, it was the brief – the instructions from the client contained in a specific letter – in this case from a teacher suspended from her post for teaching evolution theory, which really worked to hook the pupils, in their roles as junior lawyers, into the main thrust of this task-based drama. A major objective of this drama was the continuous production of pupil-generated sign – to be used as evidence in the final hearing.

From the key examples, we can see that the teacher, in each case, generated a number of different items with which to sign the drama. However, if we look into this a little more we can see there are actually three different aspects of prepared sign which each teacher created. One we have called the 'hook', another we have called 'other prepared sign' and the third we have called 'teacher sign'. This is a critical distinction and it is essential that the teacher includes each in the planning process. It is worth dwelling on this for a moment.

If we look back to Chapter 6 on Frame, we will recall that frame is the tension-giver in the drama and that this tension is directly related to the learning area. If we follow this through to our consideration of sign, we will see that in process drama sign demonstrates in a physical and symbolic way the tension which is provided by the frame.

Sign Grid

Learning Area	Context	Pupils' role	Frame	Teacher's role	Sign (a) Hook (b) Other prepared sign (c) Teacher sign
Why people undertake long and difficult journeys in the hope of something better at the end	Victorian London	Inhabitants of London/	who are discontent with their lives in London	Shadowy role/ Ship's captain	(a) broadsheet announcing gold strike and a public meeting (b) large wall map of route between England and Australia (c) small map of Australia and a gold nugget
Can evolution theory and creation theory be reconciled?	Present day Jamaican law firm	Junior lawyers...	who have to gather evidence in four days	Head of legal firm	(a) brief from client (b) law books, documents (c) file
The horror of warfare techniques	First World War trenches in France	Soldiers...	who have no gas masks	Quartermaster	(a) instructions for using gas masks, empty gas mask box (b) ground plan of trenches on floor (c) clipboard with orders
The symbolic representation of war and the role of women in war	Post-First World War artists studio	Sculptors...	whose designs have been rejected for not including the role of women	Cleaning lady	(a) rejection letter (b) studio 'clutter', sculpture designs (c) cleaning materials
Taking plant species from an environment impacts negatively on the local people	Present day briefing at the Ministry of Agriculture	Botanists...	who must keep their expedition to the rainforest secret	Civil servant from the ministry	(a) photograph of rare plants (b) map of region (c) requisition slips

Figure 7.3

When the teacher chooses appropriately, the things used as sign will carry within them the energy, urgency and imperative for the drama to unfold. In the Sign Grid (Figure 7.3), we have set out our three key examples and, in addition, the two First World War examples that we looked at in Chapter 6. We have included the signing for each example, this time broken down into the three categories.

Now, having looked at the grid, let's spend some time examining how each sign works in the dramas. In the first example, the sign which 'hooks' the children into the drama is a broadsheet announcing a gold strike in Australia.

This drama began with the children brainstorming and then creating individual still images which helped them to establish the dramatic context. However, it was the introduction of this document, as hook, with its careful wording, which immediately brought tension to the drama. In fact, the hook had to hold within it the potential to engage the pupils' interest in the drama by attracting their attention and curiosity.

In addition, the teacher also introduced a powerful other prepared sign through the prominent display of a map which showed both Great Britain and Australia. In the space between the two countries, the map held within it the dramatic potential for the epic journey about to unfold. However, this would unfold only over a sustained period of time. In other words, the empty space had significance which as yet the pupils might not have fully understood but which the teacher had to.

Similarly, in the second example shown on the grid, the teacher hooked the children into the drama with the presence of the client in the form of a letter and further signed the legal profession with law books and documents on the table which were to be used over time in the gathering of evidence.

The preceding examples can be described as *simple* hooks because they worked through a single sign-vehicle, namely the handbill in example one and the letter in example two. In the third example, however, the instructions for using gas masks worked together with the delayed introduction of the empty gas mask box, which should have contained the new issue for the company of soldiers. These combined to form a *compound* hook which fully established the danger of the soldiers' situation and the critical nature of the drill. The ground plan of the trenches taped to the floor indicated the confined environment in which the soldiers would have to operate over time and although a ground plan was prepared ahead of time by the teacher, it could have been created by the children at the outset of the drama as a context building strategy. The empty gas mask box acted as a complex signifier of the soldiers' predicament, heightened the dramatic tension and provided a compelling motivation to further fuel the unfolding drama.

In the fourth example, once again, the rejection letter functioned as a simple hook and linked the children immediately to the tension of the frame, while the additional studio clutter and sculpture designs signed the nature of the dramatic context which would be used over a period of time in the development of new designs.

In the final example, the picture of the plant to be collected on the expedition acted as a simple hook and linked the pupils directly to the mystery of the journey because of the strange nature of the plant. The map of the region worked in a different way to the map used in the journey to Australia. While that map was displayed from the outset, this was not the case in the rainforest expedition. In fact, the teacher held it in reserve as a means to refocus the tension of the drama away from the now established secret nature of the journey towards the difficulties of mounting a search in unknown territory. By adjusting the signification during the course of any drama, the teacher is able to continually focus and refocus the pupils' attention and their commitment to the unfolding action.

However, in all five examples, additional signing was present and was used to *convey the role of the teacher* in the drama. This is also part of the signing which the teacher must prepare before the drama begins, the map and gold nugget in example one, the file in example two, the clipboard with orders in example three and the cleaning materials in example four and the requisition forms in example five. These are all external indicators of the role the teacher would adopt in the drama but would serve largely to support the *behaviour and attitude* manifested by the role as the drama takes place.

So now five parts of the jigsaw puzzle which needs to be completed are in place. We've identified the theme, context, roles, frame and sign. What remains is to identify those drama strategies – the ways of working with performance forms – which we are going to need to make the drama happen in time and space. This leads us to the next chapter on *strategies*.

CHAPTER 8

Strategies

**Key Question:
'Which ways of working will I use? In which combination? For
what purpose?'**

If you have worked your way through the planning process as we have outlined in
the preceding chapters, you will now find yourself in the position of having to
consider the many different ways in which you and the pupils may be able to bring
the drama to life.

To help with this choice, we should spend a moment thinking again about three
theatre elements – contrast, time and space.

In Chapter 2 we talked about drama hinging on three sets of contrasts – silence
and sound, darkness and light, stillness and movement and mentioned how
meaning can be made through the friction at the interface between them.
Contrasts can be used to construct and explore environment, mood, the very
essence of the fictional circumstances under scrutiny as they unfold in space and
time. They are tools which the drama teacher has at her disposal, and which are
available to both herself and her pupils as a broad range of clearly identifiable
strategies which may be used to slow down, speed up or stop time, to create the
illusion of wide open spaces or terrible confinement, to demonstrate social
position and power or lack of it, to listen to people's innermost thoughts and
connect with their feelings as well as a host of other things. These contrasting
elements are what the teacher uses to mould dramatic form.

But as we have already mentioned, there is a wide range of strategies or
performance forms available through which the teacher can mould the form of the
drama – to make it come to life. The key to success here is knowing which
strategies to use at which point, in which combination and for which purpose.

This is very important. It might seem, for example, that deciding that the pupils
will pretend to be paddling down the river towards the first cataract of the Nile,
and having the class of 35 children sitting on the hall floor in lines of five or six,
one behind the other, shuffling along on their bottoms, is the obvious way in

which a drama about ancient Egypt might be brought to life. However, the result of this decision is actually likely to reduce the class to giggling and rolling around on the floor – not a desirable situation for the teacher!

The outcome of this will be to shatter the tension of the drama and the commitment of the pupils to what is happening because this literal approach is clearly inappropriate to these dramatic circumstances.

'Why is it inappropriate?'

At first glance, the teacher does seem to have brought the situation to life. After all, in our discussion of teacher-in-role, we stressed that process drama has whole-group improvisation at its heart. We are not contradicting ourselves here. Whole-group improvisation with TIR *is* one of the key ways of working in process drama. However, it is not the *only* way and neither is it always the best way. In fact, there is a rich variety of drama strategies available and the teacher needs to recognise and understand them in order to choose the one that is going to make any particular part of the drama happen, *most meaningfully*.

'What do you mean?'

Well, in considering which strategies to use at different points in the drama, we need to remember that we are working in an art form. Drama works within a fictional framework and so perhaps can never really be 'accurate'. So, the children shuffling along on their bottoms cannot give an accurate portrayal of fighting rapids on a mighty river. However, when working in drama we need to recognise that while we cannot recreate 'accurately', we need always to strive to create 'meaningfully'. This engages us with aesthetic considerations.

Creating the negotiation of the rapids through whole-group improvisation is unlikely to be successful because this strategy brings the pupils too close to their own play behaviour. It works against any possibility of maintaining the carefully nurtured and developed commitment created earlier in the drama, by breaking the suspension of disbelief – the pupils become themselves again, playing at paddling a canoe, and dramatic tension is lost.

However, if we take the same situation again, we can perhaps see how the outcome can be very different – and more successful and meaningful – by evoking this part of the drama through a different drama strategy. For example, the teacher could enable the pupils like this:

- divide the pupils into groups of four or five;
- each group, out of role, works out the story of their canoe's journey down the river;

- each group chooses the most important, exciting or dangerous moment of that journey;
- each group makes a still image or tableau of that moment;
- each person decides on one line of dialogue that they were saying which sums up how they were feeling/what they were thinking at that moment;
- in turn, each group presents its frozen moment, including the dialogue, as the teacher plays a recording of the sound of a raging and dangerous river.

'What does this give the drama that the other strategy doesn't?'

To begin with, being in a smaller working group helps the pupils to focus on the implications of the dramatic context – it makes them think about the fictional situation and gives them time to reflect on what it might actually be like. It also provides the opportunity for the teacher to move between the groups and help the pupils in their task; the use of still image precipitates the pupils into finding the essence of the dramatic moment rather than dissipating it; it allows a greater input from each pupil and it encourages the possibility of a greater emotional connection to the event by challenging them to crystallise the feelings of the archaeologists in this perilous situation. It also provides the means by which all of the pupils in the class can *see* what happened to everyone else on the journey, so strengthening the fabric of the drama itself.

From this example we hope that you will see that choice of appropriate strategies is as important a planning element as all those that we have mentioned so far. This means that the teacher will have to address her choice of drama strategies very carefully.

'Could you explain more about these drama strategies?'

Drama strategies are the different performance forms which, when combined, build and make the process drama happen in action.

At the beginning of this book, and at different points throughout it, we have made reference to the elements of theatre – focus, metaphor, tension, symbol, contrast, role, time and space, which we stated were common to all forms of drama experience. Drama strategies, therefore, encapsulate in their different forms, these same key elements of theatre. So, if we return to the river example, we can see that the reason the first example fell apart at the seams was because the inappropriate choice of 'whole-group improvisation' led to the elements of role and tension being lost.

But we can also see from the river example that different parts of a process drama can be 'acted out' in different ways. There is a common pool of performance forms available from which different theatre genres may draw. These forms can be combined together in a wide variety of ways to enrich, enliven and deepen the quality of the drama experience. So, when the teacher chooses strategies – performance forms – from an informed position, understanding what each can offer to the structure of the drama and, therefore, to the experience of the pupils, she is able to create dramas which provoke stimulating thought and discussion; and precipitate the participants into action.

Well-crafted process dramas engage participants emotionally, kinaesthetically and cognitively by providing opportunities to develop new perspectives and insights through an empowering framework for the exploration of ideas, feelings and the making of meaning. The choice of appropriate strategy at each point as the drama unfolds, added to the choice of learning area, context, role, frame and sign is, in our view, the means by which such well-crafted process dramas are made.

'So where do these appropriate strategies come from?'

There is a range of performance forms available to establish the context, move the narrative forward, explore and deepen the meaning and provide the opportunity to reflect upon the experience for the audience. In process drama we need to make different parts of the drama happen in different ways to maximise the learning opportunities for the children so that they make meaning for themselves.

Let's explore this a bit more. When we watch a staged play as part of an external audience, we may observe actors who narrate sections of the story while it is being enacted by others. Or a soliloquy may allow us to hear what's going on in a character's mind. An aside may startle us as a character appears to step out of the action of the play and communicate directly with the audience rather than with other characters on stage. Action may be mimed, dialogue conducted between characters, sound effects used to create moods and atmosphere. As members of a watching audience, we've become familiar with a whole range of theatre forms and skilled in reading them in order to extract meaning from them.

As we have said earlier, in process drama there is no watching audience, but the internal audience is always present and we need to draw upon this wealth of theatre forms in this genre, too, in order to make meaning for that audience – that is, the participants themselves.

'How many strategies are available for a drama teacher to use?'

There are numerous drama strategies, or performance forms, available and Jonothan Neelands and Tony Goode have categorised and set out written descriptions of 72 key conventions in their book, *Structuring Drama Work*, which is an excellent resource (see Further reading section). It is important for drama teachers to be familiar with the range of strategies available to them. The more they have at their command, the more sophisticated the dramas they construct with their pupils will be.

However, grasping them all and knowing when to use them and what effect they will have upon the drama, will obviously take time. It would be unreasonable to expect a teacher to have a complete grasp of the whole repertoire of available theatre forms from the outset. We believe that any teacher must build that repertoire of strategies, as must the pupils, for it is in this area that both pupils and teachers will learn most about what theatre form can do within process drama. It is in using a range of drama strategies that pupils and teachers, like all good theatre practitioners, will continue to explore, test and stretch the boundaries of the art form.

'Can I get a list?'

We've already referred to an excellent book and offer guidance on further reading at the end of this book but our advice is to start with a basic tool kit and add to it as you become more confident. One way of developing a repertoire of strategies to use in process drama is, first of all, to identify what ways of working are familiar to you already. Potential ways of working may not only be drawn from the performance forms of formal western theatre, but are to be found in all sorts of performance traditions. So, whatever cultural tradition you are working in it's a good idea to note down some of its performance forms.

- Are there any folk forms with which you are familiar?
- Are there songs which tell stories or commemorate people or events within the community?
- Is there a storytelling tradition?
- Are there any rituals, ceremonies, festivals or carnivals in your community?
- Are there any dance forms to which you could turn for inspiration?
- Are there special costumes for important occasions?
- Is there a tradition of masks and/or puppetry?
- Are there special art and craft skills associated with performance – for example, straw weaving, painting, costume building?

In addition, you may see live theatre performances from time to time. Have you ever seen any techniques or conventions used in these theatre performances which you could make use of with your pupils? Some of the strategies most frequently used in process drama and other theatre genres have emerged from social settings (meetings, interviews, telephone conversations); technology (rewinding or fast-forwarding the action, sound tracks, slow-motion and sound effects); changing the numbers involved (pair work, whole-group improvisation, small group playmaking); children's games (freeze/still image, ring play and other formations). You may very quickly find yourself accumulating a range of useful performance forms which can be invaluable to you in your drama work. What is important to remember is that these performance forms are, in effect, simply different ways of presenting human experience.

But before we go any further, let's consider the different categories or *sorts* of strategy you will need at your disposal. Different strategies actually serve different purposes and in order to build a well-crafted drama you'll need to recognise the different types of purpose you'll need, and to recognise which strategy serves which purpose.

'What do you mean by strategies serving a purpose?'

When we look into how a drama is structured we can see that the nature of what is happening does not remain constant. In order to create the drama and move the story on so that the participants gain from the experience in the way that we hope, we have to recognise that strategies will need to do different things.

Choosing the right kinds of drama strategies allows us to ensure that the drama becomes of the highest quality possible. For example, there will be times when we need strategies which will build the dramatic context. That is to say, once we have decided on the dramatic context in which the drama will unfold, we have to find means by which to make it concrete for the pupils. We may wish to do this by defining or redefining the space in which the drama is unfolding and this could be achieved by rearranging the furniture to suggest the desks and chairs of a travel agency; or by marking out the trenches of The First World War with masking tape on the floor; or by creating a palace wall made up of everyone in the class. But, defining the space will not be the only strategy available for establishing the dramatic context. The teacher may be more concerned, initially, with individual pupils' 'sense of belonging' to a group in the dramatic context and so she may have them drawing or writing in role, making badges or filling in forms. Whichever strategy she chooses, it will serve its purpose in the development of the drama (in this case, the building of the dramatic context), in a particular way.

Shifting into the main body of the story or 'narrative' being created in the drama will mean shifting to new strategies which allow the drama to develop and unfold in a different way. In our First World War example, this may mean shifting to an 'overheard conversation', perhaps having the soldiers overhear officers discussing the shortage of gas masks, or to a 'meeting' where the soldiers meet to decide how best to prepare for a potential gas attack. Such shifts of strategy facilitate a move into the main body of the action of the story, development of a greater awareness and understanding of the issues and problems of the circumstances of the drama.

Opportunities for pupils engaging with the deeper emotional or symbolic aspects of the drama may be introduced through a further shift towards strategies which deepen the experiences through the affective power of the art form. For example, pupils as soldiers might write what may be their last letters home or write as if they were war poets.

Finally, 'giving witness' as survivors of a trench gas attack at a tribunal after the war represents yet another shift which now presents the pupils with the opportunity to reflect seriously on the full implication of the drama in a manner which is meaningful and not superficial.

What we have just described does not amount to a complete lesson plan but it does give an indication of the ways in which a careful application of selected performance forms serves to move forward and deepen the experience of the drama for pupils.

'It seems as if different stategies work in different ways. Is this so?'

Neelands and Goode classified strategies as 'context building', 'narrative building', 'poetic' and 'reflective' and drama teachers everywhere have found this classification very helpful. It is, therefore, well worth thinking about the functions different types of strategy can serve in a process drama. They can, generally speaking, serve four different purposes. It is most often the case that well-crafted and therefore successful dramas are structured in a way which incorporates different strategies which serve all four purposes in order to give pupils as deep and complete an experience as possible. So, let's give some attention to examining the four types of strategy.

Put simply, as a teacher you will find that you need strategies to:

(a) establish the dramatic context;
(b) move the story of the drama forward;
(c) explore a greater depth of meaning and feeling;
(d) help the pupils to reflect on the drama.

To start with, it is essential that you equip yourself with a basic 'tool kit' of drama strategies and then add to it as you become more confident.

We don't necessarily subscribe to the view that particular strategies may only be used for specific purposes, for example, context building *only*. Depending on the teacher's intention, some strategies can be used as different forms of action and can also serve more than one purpose at once.

Let's try to pull together a basic tool kit of drama strategies by once again looking at our key examples. For each of these we have drawn up the complete list of strategies used in the development of the dramas and briefly outlined the elements of the narrative which were carried by each strategy.

Key Example 1 – 6/7-year-olds

Theme/ Learning Area	*Context*	*Pupils' roles*	*Frame*	*Sign*
taking plant species from an environment impacts negatively on the local people	present day briefing at the Ministry of Agriculture	botanists who... *Teacher's role* civil servant from the ministry	must keep their expedition to the rainforest secret	photograph of rare plant, secrecy pact, writing materials, clipboard, requisition slips

Strategies used

1. Out of role discussion – what is a botanist?
2. Teacher-in-role – civil servant from the Ministry of Agriculture.
3. Whole-group improvisation – a confidential meeting of botanists at the Ministry – teacher-in-role introduces the secret expedition.
4. Ritual – signing of the secrecy agreement.
5. Small groups – deciding on what equipment to take.
6. Small groups – deciding on cover story for travelling to Brazil.
7. Whole-group improvisation with teacher-in-role – getting through immigration at the airport.
8. Meeting with teacher-in-role – deciding which route to take to the search area.
9. Group still images – the highlight of your journey through the rainforest.
10. Group narratives – each group's story of their journey to the meeting point – reporting sightings of plant en route.
11. Pictogram – message in pictures from the rainforest dwellers.
12. Whole-group improvisation with teacher-in-role – deciphering the message and deciding what to do as the plant is medicine for the rainforest dwellers.
13. Pair work – devising a sign language to communicate with the rainforest dwellers.
14. Teacher-in-role (as a person from the rainforest) and pair work – communicating the message.
15. Whole-group improvisation – agreeing a compromise solution to the problem.
16. Whole-group improvisation with teacher-in-role as Minister – facing the music.
17. Small group work – press conference.
18. Group still images – photographic record of the key moments of the expedition.

Key Example 2 – 8/9-year-olds

Theme/ Learning Area	*Context*	*Pupils' roles*	*Frame*	*Sign*
what makes human beings give up what they know and take a long and difficult journey in the hope of something better at the end?	Victorian London as gold find in Australia is announced	inhabitants of London who... *Teacher's role* ship's captain	are discontent with their lives in London	broadsheet announcing gold strike and a public meeting, large wall map of route between England and Australia, small map of Australia, gold nugget

Strategies used

1. Brainstorm of why people leave where they are living and go on a long and difficult journey in the hope of something better at the other end.
2. Individual still image – moment of contentment with life in London.
3. Individual still image – same role – moment of discontentment with life in London.
4. Pair conversations – tell partner why discontent.
5. Teacher in shadowy role – spreading news of gold strike and meeting in town hall about ship going to Australia – pairs discussing this news.
6. Whole-group improvisation – public meeting – teacher-in-role as Captain of ship.
7. Group still image – the moment the groups decided to go.
8. Reading the images – who is happy, who is the powerful one, what is the relationship between the people in the groups.
9. Writing in role – diary entries that night – place on map on wall near London.
10. Whole-group improvisation with teacher-in-role on the quayside signing up for passage – TIR stressing can't take much on board.
11. Drawing in role – keepsakes – tell others near you what it is and why it is precious to you – add to map on wall.
12. Individual mime – packing your small case of personal belongings.
13. Still images plus thought-tracking – what is going through your mind as you leave for the ship – speak, then move to meeting point.
14. Whole-group improvisation with TIR – getting on board.

15. Polaroid photos of each group at foot of gangway – write group caption for picture summing up group feelings – put on map.
16. Writing in role – diary entries, first night on ship – put on map.
17. Small group playmaking – the first thing to go wrong.
18. Sharing the incidents – named by the whole group – place of incident marked on map and name written on.
19. Out of role, one incident selected by whole group to explore consequences – outbreak of infectious disease.
20. Whole-group improvisation with TIR – ship meeting to decide what to do.
21. Ritual – burial at sea – thought-tracking as body is buried.
22. Writing in role – diary entry, that night – add to map around point where incident was marked.
23. Celebration – ship free from disease. Storytelling of other celebrations attended – trying to guess what Australia will be like – what to do with the gold when found.
24. Storm at sea – out of role decide story of what happened to your travelling group in your part of the ship during storm.
25. In role – group still image of most important or dangerous moment of the story.
26. Add two more images – one a few moments before and another a few moments after.
27. Put together in series of three still images.
28. Add a line of dialogue for each person in each image.
29. Bring still images to life in slow motion and string together in continuous sequence of movement – add dialogue.
30. Whole class shares storm sequences consecutively – rest of class creating sounds of storm when not showing their episode.
31. Ceremony – giving thanks for salvation from the storm.
32. Writing in role – diary entries, that night – add to the map at the location of the storm.
33. Arrival in Australia – disembarking from the ship – teacher narration and whole-class mime of gathering belongings.
34. Photographs of disembarkation – polaroids – add caption and add to map.
35. Writing in role – letters home – add to map.
36. Whole-group improvisation – meeting to decide what to do about getting to gold fields – three possible routes – which way to go? Debating the pros and cons – stick together or separate – children decided to stick together.
37. Writing in role – diary entries, that night.
38. Journey through the mountains – using same strategy as for the storm at sea.

39. Arrival in the gold fields – whole-group improvisation with TIR – taking leave of each other as we separate to stake our claims.
40. Staking claims and finding gold – group mime and teacher narration.
41. Writing in role – diary entries, that night.
42. Teacher narration and small group mime – finding gold.
43. Writing in role – letters home telling of conditions and success.
44. Marking the moment – individually go to that part of the map which shows the most important part of the drama for you and sharing with the others the reasons for your choice.
45. Monument to the Gold Seekers – reflection on journey – in groups create a statue which symbolises the experiences of the travellers – add an inscription to go round plinth – share with other groups – polaroids of statues – add to the map.

Key Example 3 – 11/13-year-olds

Theme/ Learning Area	*Context*	*Pupils' roles*	*Frame*	*Sign*
creation theory versus evolution theory–why does a tension exist between those who hold different views about the origins of life on earth?	present day Jamaican law firm gathering evidence for a case	lawyers who... *Teacher's role* head of law chambers	need to meet a deadline to present evidence for the official hearing	brief from client, law books, documents, file

Strategies used
1. Teacher-in-role as senior partner with law firm briefs legal team about new case.
2. Teacher-in-role reads letter from a teacher seeking legal assistance. She has been dismissed from her post for teaching evolution theory, against the expressed wishes of the school governors, who had instructed her to teach creation theory and to be guided by the account of the creation as set down in the Old Testament.

3. Brainstorming in role about what kinds of evidence to present at a projected hearing, which would be in the best interests of the client, without necessarily further alienating the governors of the school.

4. Decision made to present a 'balanced' body of evidence, with suggestions for different types of approaches which might be taken in the gathering of evidence in this case.

5. Dividing up into smaller groups for gathering and development of specific types of evidence.

6. Introduction to selection of useful research literature, information, materials, etc.

7. Opportunities for question and answer sessions, interviews and interaction with resource persons including qualified anthropologist, choreographer, visual artist, etc.

8. Daily meetings in role to monitor the progress of the work.

9. Choreographing a 'creation' dance after completing a cross-cultural comparison of creation stories and myths of origin.

10. Assembly, in role, of a large collage mural on primate evolution depicting Australopithecus, Homo Erectus, Cro-magnon man, Homo Sapiens, etc.

11. Construction, in role, of a three-dimensional model of a Pterodactyl as a hanging mobile.

12. Installation, in role, of a life-size, two-dimensional outline of a Tyrannosaurus Rex on the side of a two-storey building.

13. Development and construction, in role, of an interactive model of plate tectonics.

14. Choosing, in role, a suitable scale and producing of a geological time line representing approximately 400 million years of the Earth's history.

15. Designing and producing, in role, the models for a dinosaur diorama.

16. Small group site meetings at the work stations for each of the evidence gathering projects.

17. Presenting evidence in role as junior counsel at the final hearing.

18. Symbolic, ritualised depiction of creation in dance/drama form.

19. Attempting, in role, to reconcile the opposing views presented by both sides in this argument.

From our key examples, we have compiled a list of those strategies which we think would serve well as a basic strategy tool kit. This represents a core sample only of the available forms and you may well find that you will want to add others to your particular list. However, those drawn from our key examples are:

- Brainstorming
- Captioning in photographs
- Mime
- Narration

- Ceremony
- Defining the space
- Drawing in role
- Folk forms
- Group sculpting
- Group still image
- Individual still image
- Maps and diagrams
- Marking the moment
- Meeting
- Pictogram

- Pair work
- Reading images
- Ritual
- Slow motion
- Small group playmaking
- Sound effects
- Storytelling
- Teacher-in-role
- Thought-tracking
- Whole-group improvisation
- Writing in role

Clearly, in the early stages of your working with process drama, you will find yourself more comfortable with some strategies than others. It is sensible to walk before you can run, and therefore steadily build up your repertoire – especially as some strategies are more complex than others. The most important factor is knowing clearly about the strategies you intend to use, and the purpose you intend them to serve, in advance of the lesson. Extending your repertoire of strategies is important, not only because this will make you a more flexible teacher, able to respond more subtly to the unfolding drama, but this is essential in order that you are able to introduce your pupils to an ever growing body of performance forms, which is the key to their developing understanding of the nature of process drama.

'But how will I know when to introduce a new strategy into a lesson?'

As we have already suggested, the sequence of building a process drama tends to move through the four different types of strategy – context building, narrative building, deepening the experience and reflection on the drama. While following this sequence is a good rule of thumb, especially in small scale dramas, it should not be seen as inflexible. It may well be that it is appropriate to move back and forth between the different types of strategy.

'Won't this disrupt the story?'

Well, perhaps this would be a good point to mention about the episodic nature of process drama. We would all agree, we are sure, that drama could be described as stories in action. This might lead us to suppose that events in the drama have to unfold in a chronological order. However, this is certainly not the case, just as it is not always the case in stories, and in fact if we do always stick to a mono-directional time sequence we will miss a great opportunity to construct a tight and engaging drama and restrict the pupils' opportunity to explore the issues of the drama in as full a manner as might otherwise be possible. The episodic nature of drama liberates us from chronological sequence.

'It would help if you went over an example in more detail'

To try to illustrate this a little more clearly we will expand on the breakdown of Key Example 2, the strategies for which we have already outlined earlier.

If we look in greater detail at this analysis of the drama centred on the Australian Gold Rush, we can see a wide range of strategies in use at different times, serving different functions in the drama and, sometimes, a strategy serving more than one. What follows is a step by step breakdown of how the strategies were used as the drama unfolded over the ten sessions, with an explanation of why the teacher did as she did.

Analysis of the drama

Let's begin by reminding ourselves of some of the key elements of process drama.

Process drama can be defined largely in terms of the absence of a formal written text or script. In process drama this will be 'created in action' as the drama unfolds.

In Chapter 1 we argued that there are three broad areas of learning – personal and social, cross-curricular and about the art form, which spring from engagement in process drama. In Key Example 2, the Australian Gold Rush, we will see that both Strand A learning and Strand B learning are in balance. The teacher intended that the children (a) examine an area of human experience and (b) explore aspects of drama form. In addition, personal and social learning emerges from the activity as, for example, the nature of discontentment; making life-altering decisions; writing; understanding feelings; sentiment; making private thoughts public; vocal and physical engagement and expression; drawing, planning, problem-solving and so on.

Key Example 2

Session 1
1. **Brainstorm** of reasons why people leave where they are living and go on a long and difficult journey in the hope of something better at the other end.

Context Building

Here the pupils have the opportunity to discuss together and then share with the group their own understanding and opinions about why people move location and how they feel about it. It is surprising how much understanding of this children do have. In this age of culturally diverse and mobile populations, especially in inner-city areas, many children have real life, family experiences of relocation. In fact, the class involved in the Gold Rush drama reflected a broad range of just such family experiences. Here is just a selection of the pupils' collective understanding about what motivates people to relocate: better housing, better climate, religious persecution, adventure, political instability, employment prospects, marriage, historical connections, joining family members, being a fugitive.

2. Individual still image – moment of contentment with life in London.
Context Building
3. Individual still image – same role – moment of discontentment with life in London.
Context Building

Having brought motivations to the forefront of the pupils' thinking, what follows allows the pupils to begin to construct in their imaginations the concrete circumstances in which the first part of the drama will unfold. Having been asked by the teacher to imagine that they lived in London in the early 1850s, they are able to capture a moment of their lives there. Although it would have been possible to create just a moment of discontentment, by creating the contented moment *first*, the contrast between it and what follows throws the discontentment into higher relief, making it more meaningful. And because the pupils have already brainstormed reasons for relocation, the teacher has ensured that they are equipped with something on which to base the second still image.

4. Pair conversations – tell partner why discontent.
Narrative Building
5. Teacher in shadowy role – as an undefined member of the public distributing the handbill (the hook – refer to Chapter 5) and excitedly spreading news of gold strike and meeting in town hall about ship going to Australia – **pairs** discussing this news.
Narrative Building
6. Whole-group improvisation – public meeting – **teacher-in-role** as Captain of ship and **map** of projected route from England to Australia. The Captain extols the opportunities to be taken if the Londoners will take the risk of going to Australia and promise to pay him a percentage

of any gold they find. The meeting questions him closely about motives, risks, rewards, etc.

Context/Narrative Building

This sequence of narrative building action is deliberately constructed by the teacher to ensure that the culminating public meeting is as effective and affective as possible. By firstly encouraging the pupils to struggle to articulate their discontentment in a relatively private conversation with just one other person, the teacher has protected them into the initial establishment of a role and is priming them for their more public participation in the meeting. The next step involves the teacher taking on a role which is not fully developed, what Dorothy Heathcote has called a 'shadowy role'. This serves, largely, as a device which injects information into the drama so that it can develop further without needing to interrupt the action. It also provides the teacher with a means of activating the frame tension of the drama and the opportunity to model language and emotional engagement for the pupils. These in turn also provide resources to support the pupils in the forthcoming public meeting. The final step in this narrative building sequence is the public meeting in which the pupils are involved in a whole-group improvisation with teacher-in-role. This time, however, the teacher's role is very clearly defined – the Captain of the ship taking passage to Australia. Once more, the teacher is using this strategy to give information to the pupils within the context of the drama but this time in a much more substantial manner. This is possible because of the preliminary action which has prepared the pupils. The teacher's active introduction of the map at this point also helps to foreshadow the forthcoming shift in context from city to ship.

7. **Group still image** – the moment that the Londoners, in groups, decide to go to Australia.

Deepening

This is a crucial stage of the drama. By capturing the essence of the moment of decision, the still image holds within it the potential of all that is to come in the drama – life, death, riches, ruin. However, it is also a crucial moment within the lesson from the planning point of view. The teacher has already made her professional decision that this drama is about going to Australia. Therefore, all the pupils in the class must go! It would not be a good idea to allow three to stay behind in London while the others go off to seek their fortunes in the gold fields. On this occasion, the teacher manages the situation by stopping the drama at the end of the public meeting when the Captain left, having instructed those willing to take the risk to sign up the following morning – first come, first served. The pupils are asked to form groups of about four or five and to decide who they are in the drama, how they know each other, and where they are at the moment they decide to go to Australia. This serves two purposes in the structure of the drama. Firstly, it cuts out the possibility of not going. The teacher makes clear that some people may be going very reluctantly but, nonetheless, going they are. It also provides opportunity for the pupils to alter the roles they have begun to develop, if they want to.

8. Reading the images – groups present their images in turn while the others, out of role, interpret what they see – who is happy, who is the powerful one, what is the relationship between the people in the groups.

Context Building

Once the groups have created their still images, they present them to each other. The observers are invited to articulate what they see. On one level, this gives the pupils an opportunity to explore how meaning is made in drama other than through dialogue, but on the specific level of this drama it allows the contextual community of travellers to be more clearly defined. While the act of creating the images will have done this for the individual groups, it is the sharing with, and interpretation by, the others that builds the community collectively. In other words, in the dramatic context, the pupils, together, get to know who their travelling companions are, what sort of people they are and what sort of attitudes they hold. Within this knowledge lies further potential for the drama's development.

9. Writing in role – **diary entries** that night, the hopes, fears and aspirations of the travellers – these are affixed to the map on the wall near London.

Reflective

This affords the opportunity for reflection on the drama experience so far and offers a means of capturing and recording the essence of that experience.

This session uses strategies in all four categories of dramatic action: Context Building, Narrative Building, Deepening and Reflective. It is important in this first session that the pupils have a complete experience from building the context through to reflecting on the experience. However, at the outset of *any* process drama it is important to spend time creating a clearly defined context for the participants. This will pay dividends as the drama unfolds. Taking time at the beginning of a drama (or at a point in a drama where the context changes) to give pupils the opportunity to suspend disbelief, build their own investment in the drama and begin to develop a sense of ownership about the drama means that it becomes 'real' for them so that when a moment of crisis occurs, they care about it, and are motivated to do something about it. However, if the story of the drama is to develop – as it must – then we also need to employ narrative building action which will give impetus to the story. Having built the context, something must happen in it! So, in this session, time is also given to developing the narrative. However, only one Deepening strategy was used. This is to be expected at the beginning of a drama because in order to fully engage on a symbolic level with the meaning of the drama, there has to have been some drama first. It is also important that the pupils are left with a sense of closure at the end of the session and the individual reflection given by writing in role provides this. But by attaching these personal reflections to the large wall map, we begin to build our collective reflection on, and memory of, the drama. As the drama unfolds over subsequent sessions, the map becomes a means by which the drama can be held in suspended animation, as it were, until the next session begins.

Having annotated this session in great detail, we hope that it is possible to see how important it is for the teacher to change the type of strategies in order to achieve specific planning and learning objectives within the drama. The important thing is to remember that some of these will have more to do with the nature of the drama itself and others will have to do with other curriculum objectives. In reading the following session descriptions, see if you can identify their planning and learning objectives.

Session 2

10. **Whole-group improvisation** with teacher-in-role on the quayside signing up for passage – TIR stressing can't take much on board.

Context Building and Narrative Building

11. **Drawing in role** – keepsakes – tell others near you what it is and why it is precious to you – add to map on wall.

Deepening

12. **Individual mime** – packing your small case of personal belongings.

Deepening

13. **Still images plus thought-tracking** – what is going through your mind as you leave for the ship – speak, then move to meeting point.

Deepening and Reflective

14. **Whole-group improvisation with TIR** – getting on board.

Narrative Building

15. **Polaroid photos** of each group at foot of gangway – write group **caption** for picture summing up group feelings – put on map.

Deepening and Reflective

16. **Writing in role – diary entries**, first night on ship – put on map.

Reflective

In this session, considerably less time needs to be spent on context building action than in Session 1. The context of the quayside is a natural continuation of the foundation which has already been laid. More time can be given over to deepening and reflective action. This will most fully enable the pupils to engage with the enormity of their decision to leave, as well as the emotional dimension implicit within their prospective departure. Again, the combination of diary entries and the map provides both individual and collective reflection.

Session 3

17. **Small group playmaking** – the first thing to go wrong; *and*
18. **Sharing the incidents** – named by the whole group – place of incident marked on map and name written on.

Narrative Building

This session is important in moving the story forward. The journey to Australia in the nineteenth century was both long and hazardous. The challenges to people in passage were great. Developing the narrative in this part of the story ensures that the epic nature of the voyage becomes clearer to the pupils. It is important to recognise that the teacher has not decided on what these incidents are. This strengthens the children's hold on the drama – they have ownership of it – and this provides the commitment and motivation to engage with the learning inherent within the drama.

Session 4

19. **Out of role discussion** – one of the incidents selected by whole group to explore consequences – outbreak of infectious disease; *and*
20. **Whole-group improvisation with TIR** – ship **meeting** to decide what to do.

Narrative Building

21. **Ritual** – burial at sea – **thought-tracking** as body is buried.

Deepening

22. **Writing in role – diary entry** that night – add to map around point where incident was marked.

Deepening and Reflective

Narrative action moves the story forward, but the affective is at work in the deepening and reflective aspects of the drama; most notably, in this session, in the ritual of burial at sea.

Session 5
23. Celebration – ship free from disease. **Story telling** of other celebrations attended – trying to guess what Australia will be like – what to do with the gold when found.

Deepening and Reflective

24. Storm at Sea – **small group discussion** – out of role decide story of what happened to your travelling group in your part of the ship during storm.

Narrative Building

25. In role – **group still image** of most important or dangerous moment of the story; *and*
26. Add two more **still images** – one a few moments before and another a few moments after; *and*
27. Put together in series of three **still images**; *and*
28. Add a line of **dialogue** for each person in each image; *and*
29. Bring still images to life in **slow motion** and string together in continuous sequence of movement – add **dialogue**; *and*
30. Whole class **perform** storm sequences consecutively – rest of class **creating sounds** of storm when not showing their episode.

Deepening

31. Ceremony – giving thanks for salvation from the storm.

Deepening and Reflective

32. **Writing in role** – **diary entries** that night – add to the map at the location of the storm.

Reflective

In this session, there is deep engagement with the art form of drama. The storm at sea represents one of the most climactic moments of the story. It is also one of the moments which, for the teacher, holds the greatest danger of failing. If we return to what we were saying in Chapter 6 on Frame, we will recall that we have gone to some lengths to explain the necessity of ensuring that the participants in the drama have one foot on firm ground. So, in Session 1, although the pupils did not have experience of being Londoners in the nineteenth century, they all knew about feeling fed up and discontented at times. This meant that they could enter the drama with a frame of communication. However, in this session, the teacher is deliberately setting out to remove the firm ground. The frame is shifted from 'discontentment' to 'facing the dangers of a raging storm'. Fortunately, this is an experience beyond the pupils but, for the teacher, it poses the dilemma of how best to make the storm happen in a manner which will enhance the drama rather than detract from it. Whole-group improvisation, even with teacher-in-role, would not be satisfactory here. The pupils would merely invent superficially and externally without any emotional connection with experience. The result would be in danger of becoming chaotic and of loosing the hard-won structure and depth of engagement achieved by the pupils in the preceding sessions. However, by choosing to create the storm in an incremental manner using elements of performance, the teacher protects the pupils into the experience by imposing a 'real life' frame in which they have to come to grips with aspects of theatricality, e.g. slow motion, sound effects, dialogue.

Session 6

33. Arrival in Australia – disembarking from the ship – **teacher narration** and **whole-class mime** of gathering belongings.

Context Building

34. **Photographs** of disembarkation – polaroids – add **caption** and add to map.

Context Building and Deepening

35. **Writing in role** – letters home – add to map.

Reflective

36. **Whole-group improvisation and TIR** – meeting to decide what to do about getting to gold fields – three possible routes – which way to go? Debating the pros and cons – stick together or separate (the children decided to stick together).

Narrative Building

37. **Writing in role** – diary entries – feelings on the decision – add to map.

Reflective

This session sees the beginning of a new section of the drama. The teacher, therefore, needs to build the new context through the transition from the ship to the land. It is also important that the teacher helps the pupils to find a sense of completion of the first phase of the journey. So the photographs and the letters home allow them to reflect upon what has happened. It would have been possible here, instead, to have moved straight into a narrative building strategy. However, the pausing to reflect on what had happened also held within it all that was yet to come and so made the next shift, moving the story of the drama forward, all the more significant and meaningful.

Session 7

38. Journey through the mountains – using same **strategy as for the storm** at sea.

Narrative Building and Deepening

The pupils wanted their progress through the mountains to be impeded by difficulties and decided to create those difficulties – broken wagon wheels, lame horses, the loss of water barrels – by using the same way of working that had been used to make the storm at sea. This is a good example of the pupils taking full responsibility, not only for developing the story of the drama but also for the artistic decision of how to make the story come to life, and building on the techniques they had begun to develop during the storm at sea episode. The teacher's role in this session was as a facilitator helping the pupils to turn their ideas into action.

Session 8

39. Arrival in the gold fields – **whole-group improvisation with TIR** – taking leave of each other as we separate to stake our claims.

Narrative Building

40. Staking claims – **defining the space** by taping claims on floor.

Context Building

41. Writing in role – **diary entry** that night – add to map.

Reflective

42. Teacher narration and small group mime – finding gold.

Narrative Building

43. Writing in role – **letters** home telling of conditions and success.

Reflective

This session sees the culmination of the journey for the travellers. Once, again, the context of the drama changes and with that comes the need for a strategy to signal that change. This could have been done in a number of ways but the teacher's choice of 'defining the space' works on two levels. Firstly, it is an effective strategy for context building, *per se*. However, in addition to being appropriate in technical terms, it also suits the story of the drama – the need for the newcomers, literally, to stake their claim to land. So, taping the claims on the floor works at both levels simultaneously. The teacher's decision to narrate the finding of gold is significant. She recognised the need to ensure that this incident was as dramatically powerful and meaningful as possible. By drawing on her own storytelling and drama skills at this stage, she was able to endow the moment with significance and feeling.

Sessions 9 and 10

44. Out of role – **marking the moment** – individually go to that part of the map which shows the most important part of the drama for you and sharing with the others the reasons for your choice.

Reflective

45. Monument to the Gold Seekers – reflection on journey – in groups create a **statue** which symbolises the experiences of the travellers – add an **inscription** to go round plinth – share with other groups – polaroids of statues – add to the map.

Deepening and Reflective

The last two sessions of this unit of work were focused on drawing together the whole experience. This could have been achieved in a number of ways. The teacher could, for example, have chosen to end the drama in the gold fields by using 'ceremony' as a strategy to create a huge celebration to mark the finding of gold. However, if we return to the original theme or learning area for this drama, we will remember that the work was focused on 'what makes human beings give up what they know and take a long and difficult journey in the hope of something better at the end?' In essence, the drama was more concerned with the endeavour of the journey and less with the arrival and the gold – essential though these elements were to the drama. So, it was important for the overall learning goal, to find means to complete the work which gave prominence to the endurance of the travellers in the story of the drama and yet also gave the pupils opportunity to be somewhat distanced from the experience so that they could reflect on the more universal relevance of what they had done. Marking the moment out of role and sharing with the class the reasons for that moment's significance provided a reflective distance. The pupils were commenting as *themselves* on the experience of the people whom they had been *in role*. And, in creating the modern-day memorials to the travellers, the pupils were tasked with *symbolically* representing the *essence* of the experience in a way which would communicate the meaning to others who had not made the journey.

Through this detailed examination of a process drama, we have tried to make clear the factors the teacher took into consideration in order to build the drama. We also wanted to make clear the necessity of understanding the consequences of those choices in terms of how the drama develops and in terms of the challenges different strategies present to the pupils.

'It seems like a huge piece of work, I'm not sure I could plan all this'

Well, the manner in which the drama is described may well make it seem an overwhelming planning task but please remember that we have put down the drama in its entirety and you have read it all at once. In reality, of course, the entire drama was *not* planned out before the first session. Had it been, it would have been a less satisfactory experience for the pupils. The teacher, by planning every moment of every session in advance, would have cut out the possibility for any contribution by the pupils to the shape and direction of their work, so undermining one of the cornerstones of process drama. In fact, although she made the key planning decisions necessary to enable the drama to start – learning area, dramatic context, roles, frame and sign – as we have illustrated in earlier chapters, the teacher actually planned each session in the light of the one that had gone before – good practice in our view. This made the whole exercise more manageable for her, but also more effective for the pupils' learning.

As the unit of work unfolded, the teacher was able to make an informed choice of strategies, often together with the pupils, in order to bring the drama to life, *session by session.*

'Does this mean we've covered everything?'

We have now discussed each of the planning principles in turn, so, in one sense we have. If you have addressed each of them in your planning, then you are ready to put your plan into practice and bring the drama to life.

The next chapter deals with key points to help you make the drama happen.

CHAPTER 9

Making it Happen!

**Key Question:
'Am I ready to begin?'**

Well, almost! There are, however, some things still left to organise before you are quite ready, the first of which is the negotiation of the drama 'learning contract'.

'What does that mean?'

This is actually a prerequisite for engaging in process drama. It is really a way of describing the relationship between the teacher and her class and is informed by her understanding of that cornerstone of process drama which holds that learners who have a sense of ownership about their learning have a greater commitment to it and therefore gain more from it as a result.

We've already pointed out in Chapter 5 that process drama may sometimes require the teacher to renegotiate some of the ground rules of her classroom with her pupils. We have tried to stress that process drama implies a relationship between teacher and pupils which is based on a collaborative approach to the learning. It rests on a partnership in which the teacher doesn't present herself as 'the one who knows all'. Rather, the learning contract will be one which recognises that both teacher and pupils need to contribute to the creation and development of the drama and identifies the expectations of both. It imposes responsibilities on pupils and teacher alike to fulfil their parts of the bargain, but by so doing also creates the circumstances from which both parties can gain benefits. It makes clear that, if the demands of the contract are not fulfilled, *on both sides*, the drama experience will be lessened.

'I'm not sure about this'

It is quite common for teachers who are new to process drama to imagine that they need to have a whole collection of skills which they do not have at present. They

equires attributes which only a few teachers have.
:ir lack of experience in drama, especially acting, and
:y are unable to teach drama. As we stressed when
s is not true.

cular skills and attitudes which are necessary for a
to work successfully in process drama, but we would
are the skills and attitudes which are the hallmark of
centred on the view that the teacher has of herself
; – a view which sees the teacher in a learning
he teaches.

We wish to underline that teaching drama does *not* encourage any negation of responsibility on the part of the teacher. The view of drama in education as an activity in which the teacher was concerned with giving pupils carte blanche to 'express themselves' is one which no longer has currency. We will always carry the ultimate, professional responsibility for what happens in our classrooms, and we will always need to make informed decisions about the direction of our pupils learning. However, within these parameters, the type of relationship we need to develop with our pupils to create the climate in which process drama may flourish, will be one of 'colleagueness'. This climate will have an impact on the manner in which the teacher negotiates with her pupils, structures her questions to them and her responses to those they ask. If you have already established this sort of working relationship with your class you are well on your way to negotiating the drama 'learning contract'.

However, particularly if both you and your class are new to process drama, you will need to make *explicit* the contract between you. This is important for several reasons. Firstly, we are inviting pupils to have feet in two worlds simultaneously – their own real world and the fictional world of the drama – and the learning contract helps participants to recognise the boundaries of each so that they are able to behave appropriately. Secondly, the contract will ensure that everyone knows what is expected of everyone else, so strengthening the sense of the drama as a shared experience with shared benefits and shared responsibilities. Thirdly, the contract gives a point of reference for reflection upon the experience so that, as a group, it is possible to see how well everyone has lived up to the contract and how they might move forward next time.

'So how do I make the contract with the pupils?'

It might be useful to provide a short set of key points which will help you to develop the contract.

You will need to agree to

- accept that pupils will contribute meaningfully to the shape and direction of their own learning;
- be ready to withhold some of your knowledge from time to time so that the pupils can develop and demonstrate theirs;
- ask the sorts of questions which are open, and invite genuine responses from the pupils: these will often be indirect or 'musing' – 'I've often wondered about ...', 'Can anyone think of ...', 'Does anyone here have experience of this sort of situation?';
- be prepared to weave into the fabric of the drama the contributions of the pupils;
- make clear to the pupils what they are doing and why – never 'con' the pupils, accept that they need to know that it's drama;
- protect pupils into the experience by sensitive choices of material and ways of working.

The pupils will need to agree to

- accept that working in drama is serious;
- accept that each has something to offer and respect the contributions of others;
- accept that drama is about thinking and feeling as well as action;
- behave in a manner which is appropriate;
- be ready to take responsibility for helping to shape the direction of the drama.

You all will need to agree to

- a set of rules to help the drama to 'run' – for example, signals for pausing the drama;
- recognise that everyone needs to work together for the common good of the drama;
- be willing to trust each other;
- be willing to make an effort;
- be willing to take a risk within the knowledge that everyone will support the drama to develop;
- accept that you all need to develop a consensus about what is happening in the drama because the drama belongs to you all.

'Am I there, now?'

Well, by following the planning principles which we have described in the previous chapters, you will now have decided what the learning area for the drama is, having taken into account curriculum demands and the availability of time and space; the dramatic context in which it is to happen; the roles that both you and the pupils are going to take; the frame which will provide the dramatic tension and distance the pupils; the signs which you are going to use to bring significance to the drama and focus the pupils' attention on the learning area, and you will have decided on the different ways of working you are going to use. You will also have negotiated the ground rules for the work with the pupils through the drama learning contract.

As we pointed out at the end of Chapter 2, sometimes ideas will overlap or pop into your mind simultaneously or in a different planning order to the one we have set out. Although this may seem confusing, don't worry as long as you have each element included in the plan. Selection of the learning area must always come first,

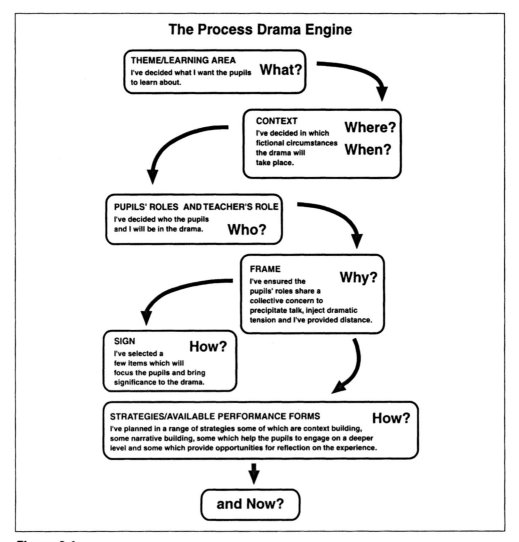

The Process Drama Engine

THEME/LEARNING AREA
I've decided what I want the pupils **What?**
to learn about.

CONTEXT
I've decided in which **Where?**
fictional circumstances
the drama will **When?**
take place.

PUPILS' ROLES AND TEACHER'S ROLE
I've decided who the pupils
and I will be in the drama. **Who?**

FRAME
I've ensured the **Why?**
pupils' roles share a
collective concern to
precipitate talk, inject dramatic
tension and I've provided distance.

SIGN **How?**
I've selected a
few items which will
focus the pupils and bring
significance to the drama.

STRATEGIES/AVAILABLE PERFORMANCE FORMS **How?**
I've planned in a range of strategies some of which are context building,
some narrative building, some which help the pupils to engage on a deeper
level and some which provide opportunities for reflection on the experience.

and Now?

Figure 9.1

but it doesn't matter if you have thought of roles before context, provided that you have chosen roles which will lead the pupils to the learning area.

However, while having all these elements in place is good, something else must happen before they become drama.

Figure 9.1 provides a construction kit with which to build the drama. If you imagine it as an engine, made up of different parts, it is now fully fuelled and ready to go but, actually, it won't go until you have added the spark plug and switched it on. This is the position you are in now. You have the engine but still need the *spark* to ignite the drama – *to make it happen*. You need to find a mechanism for switching the drama on.

To look at it in another way, you've now arrived at the moment when you say 'and now the drama is going to begin'. The big question is, 'How do I make it happen?' The answer is that you need to move into what is known as the *'now time'* of the drama.

'What does this mean?'

Well, put simply, it means that drama happens in the *present moment*. If we remember that drama can be described as ideas in action, it is obvious that action happens now, in the present moment. We can talk about what action will take place in the future; we can talk about what action has taken place in the past; but if we want to *engage* in action, if it is to happen at all, it must happen *now*.

Thinking about storytelling for a moment will really help to illustrate this point. Stories are almost always told in the past tense – the 'one time, long time ...' of Caribbean storytelling, or its European equivalent of 'once upon a time ...'. However, if others enact the story as the storyteller is telling it, while he continues to tell the story in the past tense, the enactment takes place *in the present* – the past of the story is liberated into the 'now time' of drama.

Occasionally, colloquially, someone might relate events in the present tense; for example, 'I'm going down the street, when this bloke comes up to me and starts asking the way to the fountain. Well, I'm thinking what's all this about? We haven't got one here! And he's carrying a bucket!' In this case, although the language is constructed in the present tense, the storyteller is still referring to events which took place in the past, and others enacting the story would still be engaged in releasing those past events into the 'now time' of the drama – into the present moment.

In a play, dialogue unfolds as direct speech, in a fictional context, happening now. In process drama, this has to be equally true. While there is no pre-written script, nonetheless the dialogue between the participants will be in the present moment, just as all conversation is.

'Isn't this a bit obvious?'

Well, it is and it isn't. We often expect people to instinctively know that drama unfolds in the 'now time' of a fictional construct but frequently they're not aware of what the full implications of that are for the art form. For example, in Chapter 4 we made the distinction between the real life context of the school and classroom, the general contextualisation of learning which drama can provide within education and the fictional context of the drama. These do not exist separately, but represent parallel states, if you will. When we are working in the fictional context of the drama, it is still within the real life context of the classroom, but we make a psychological and emotional shift. Similarly, the general contextualisation of learning is manifested in the particular fictional circumstances of the drama.

'So what's that got to do with "now time"?'

Well, the 'now time' of the drama exists as part of the real time of the school day but shifting into the 'now time' of the drama *alters our perception of time.*

'How, exactly, does this relate to process drama?'

Let's look at an example.

If we go back to The Vikings example that we used in Chapter 5 when we looked at context, the teacher could discuss with her class what it might have been like for the monks on Lindisfarne facing the imminent invasion. In reply to her questions, the pupils might respond like this:

Teacher:	'What do you think the monks could see?'
Pupils:	'The long ships would be on the horizon.'
	'They might see fierce people with swords.'
	'There would be a row of shields on the side of the boat.'
	'They might see nothing if it was dark, miss.'
Teacher:	'How do you think the monks would be feeling?'
Pupils:	'Scared, miss.'
	'Worried.'
	'They might be worried about what the Vikings will steal.'

This type of conversation talks *about* the situation but there is a world of difference between this and:

'Brethren, lock the church door, we have little time'

because this *shifts the drama into the now time* of the fictional circumstance. We are no longer talking about it – we are there in it, it is happening to us, now! In effect, the drama has begun. This is an absolutely critical concept. While discussing or brainstorming ideas with the class could be useful activities which would inform the drama by helping the pupils to focus on the content of the drama, if they only ever talk about it, the drama will never happen.

We referred earlier to the storyteller telling the story in the past tense but with its simultaneous enactment in the present moment. This alteration of our perception places us squarely within the time frame and experience of the story. The possibility of our effecting this shift into the 'now time' of the drama opens up a host of different possibilities. Language holds within it many different tenses to which we relate from our position in the present. In real circumstances we can neither relive the past nor experience the future – yet we can refer to them in language and even go so far as to speculate as to what might have been, or what might be in the future. The 'now time' of the drama is an enormously powerful tool simply because it holds within it the potential to release us into a 'spectrum of presents' or 'new reals'. The learning which comes about in process drama (both about the art form and through it) is not achieved in the simplistic improvising of a 'now' situation but by using the possibilities inherent within that 'now' to explore dramatically:

- this is how it was
- this is how it might have been
- this is how it may be
- this is how it will be
- this is how it ought to be
- this is how it should have been
- this is how it could have been
- this is how it usually is
- this is how it usually was
- this is how we would like it to be

but all experienced as 'now'.

So when the teacher shifts the pupils, in the example given above, from the mere speculation of 'they might see fierce people with swords' to 'Brethren, lock the church door, we have little time', a switch has been thrown which catapults the participants immediately into the direct perception of a 'so this is what it was like' situation – *only it's happening now.*

'But will the pupils really know what's going on if you say, "Brethren, lock the door"?'

Well, they certainly won't, if it is said out of context, with no preparation. But we have already indicated that a preparatory discussion or other context building activities would be desirable. Indeed, we really do believe that it is vital to keep the pupils informed about what's going on. Pupils need to know what they are doing and this includes knowing that what they are doing is drama and that it is not 'real', *even if it feels real.* And it is precisely because it does feel real that it is a good idea to tell the pupils that the drama is going to begin and not suddenly spring things on them. While this may not seem like a big problem with a drama about something so obviously historical as The Vikings, it is, and even more so, if the drama is focused on a contemporary issue such as bullying, racism or pollution, when it might be more difficult for the pupils to see the boundary between the fictional and real contexts.

However, we are *not* suggesting that you need to plot out every aspect of the drama before it unfolds. As we have pointed out, process drama is fundamentally an improvised form and there has to be scope within it for the contribution of the participants. The development by the pupils of a sense of ownership about their learning, you will remember, is one of the cornerstones of process drama. Moreover, if the teacher decides everything that is going to happen in the session, not only does she work against the development of this sense of ownership but places a limit on the scope for creative and imaginative input by the pupils and unforeseen development in dramatic tension.

So, prior to the cry 'Brethren, lock the church door...' the teacher may have conducted a brainstorming session similar to the one above; used still images to build the scene on the island prior to the ships being sighted; she might have used recorded plain chant to evoke the atmosphere of the monastery; indeed, she might have combined all of these strategies to build the context of the drama.

However, when, as teacher-in-role, she addresses the assembled monastic community and says, 'Lock the church door, we have little time', something fundamental takes place. The drama is brought into existence because she has made it happen *now,* and those 'fierce people with swords' are now created as '*absent others*' who, in turn, create the artistic process of the self-spectator. In other words, the 'absent others' (in this case the Viking invaders) make us see 'us behaving' (as monks under threat of siege) and selecting choices (one of which is locking the church door). So in throwing the switch which propels us into the discourse of the drama, it is the attitude, language and stance of the teacher which is essential.

'Could you say more about this attitude, language and stance?'

Suppose we think again about something we mentioned in Chapter 6 on Frame. You will recall that we talked about the teacher's aim of moving pupils from the known to the unknown so that they gain new insights and shifts of perceptions, and that we emphasised how successful process drama is in enabling this to happen. However, you will also remember that an important consequence of this is that teachers will be constantly asking pupils to step onto the shaky ground of the unknown. One of the mechanisms for helping the participants into this experience, as we pointed out, was to select a communication frame which had an element of familiarity from the pupils' real life experiences – loss, secrecy, time constraints.

However, there is another powerful set of tools that the teacher has at her disposal and which she can use to ignite the drama and support her pupils into 'now time'. These are the attitude, language and stance, together with the body language she adopts when moving into teacher-in-role.

If we again look back to our discussion of frame as the means by which dramatic tension is created in process drama, we will recall that it is possible to do this in three distinct ways and that the last two directly involve teacher-in-role.

- Through the differences in opinion between the pupils' roles – 'I think we should negotiate with the strangers', 'No, I think we should run', 'I think there may be something in this for me'.
- Through the differences between the pupils' roles and the teacher-in-role – 'You'll all have to work overtime and for less money', 'But my family can't survive on what you pay now'.
- Through the differences between the collective view of the pupils' and teacher-in-role, together, and an absent antagonist – 'What are we going to do to get past the monster?'

With the attitude of her role she is able to present something with which, or against which, the pupils can react and through the language she selects she can provide a model which the pupils can follow.

So, 'Brethren, lock the church door, we have little time', spoken by teacher-in-role as one of the monks, does two things. Firstly, it creates frame (through the differences between the collective view of the pupils and teacher-in-role, together, and an absent antagonist). Secondly, the structure of the language draws a different style of discourse from the pupils than would 'Quick, they're nearly here!'

It is for this reason that we firmly believe that *teacher-in-role is central to process drama* and should not be regarded merely as just one among the wide number of drama strategies available. As we have already seen in Chapter 5, teacher-in-role enables the teacher to operate strategically from within the drama and so negotiate and renegotiate circumstances within the fiction in order to enhance learning opportunities. A critical component of that negotiation will be negotiating the shifts into the 'now time' of the drama.

'You've said earlier that there will be lots of different strategies used in a drama. But if we are living it through as if it is happening now, how can I change strategies?'

It is important to realise that drama can stop and start. Just because it is enacted in the present moment doesn't mean that it has to be a long, continuous, uninterrupted process. In fact, it is desirable that it's not! There are going to be times when you wish to change strategy in order to move the story of the drama forward, to change the context of the drama, to deepen the experience, to reflect upon what has gone on or prepare for what is to come. If we think again about process drama being *episodic* in nature this should help to clarify this point.

If we restrict ourselves to the drama moving forward in a chronological, linear fashion, we are limiting the opportunities for the pupils to gain the maximum benefit from the experience both in terms of learning about the process drama genre and about other things through the drama.

However, if we think of process drama as a sequence of linked episodes then we are liberated to explore the substance of the drama from a range of different perspectives, to move forwards, backwards and sideways in time, change role, miss out aspects of the story which do not readily lend themselves to dramatisation. Actually, this is precisely what playwrights frequently do. They change scenes, they allow the audience to see events through the eyes of different characters, they warp time and space and allude to events which would be impractical or undesirable to present in performance. Given that – as we have stressed throughout – process drama is a theatre genre in which the teacher and pupils together 'write' the play as it unfolds in action, we should not be surprised that episodic progression applies equally to process drama.

'Is this episodic thing really so important?'

Actually, yes it is. As we've just pointed out, it allows the teacher to stop the drama, for both the pupils and herself to come out of role, change the time, place and roles and alter the strategies being used, reflect upon what has happened and plan what to do next. This may mean moving the story of the drama forward in time, but it could equally be about revisiting what has happened to examine the consequences of alternative decisions and courses of action, to see events from the viewpoint of other roles, to explore what was happening simultaneously elsewhere. The episodic structure creates freedom to slow down and even reverse the inexorable march of time. This gives the teacher the means by which she is able to stretch and challenge the pupils to engage more deeply with the substance of the drama and gain changes in perceptions and understandings. The ability to warp time in this fashion is one of the keys to successful learning in process drama.

'Can you say more about time?'

Well, let's come back to the notion that drama is a form of story. The curiosity which is one of the key features of human nature, leads us all to want to know the end of the story, whether the 'story' is a piece of gossip, half-overheard; a breaking news item; *Harry Potter; Rumpelstiltskin; Hamlet* or the next episode of a soap opera like *Eastenders*. Pupils engaged in process drama are no different in their response to the unfolding story of the drama. Like us all, they are driven to know what happens in the end. Moreover, if we don't find out the end of the story, somehow we feel cheated; we feel disconcerted and unsettled. We miss the feeling of satisfaction which we get from learning how things turned out.

Recognising this basic instinct can really help us as teachers to hone the way we shape process dramas. It helps to make clear to us that we have a sort of juggling act going on, or perhaps a tug-of-war is a better analogy.

On the one hand, we have the momentum to get to the end of the story which is fuelled by the pupils' natural curiosity about what happens next. On the other, we have our teacherly desire to challenge the pupils to really get to grips with the learning by getting down below the surface of the material. The dilemma is that the first can make it more difficult to achieve the second!

'What's this got to do with time and episodes?'

Two things, really. Firstly, it has an impact on how long a process drama lasts. It is perfectly possible to structure a process drama which is a one-off lesson. Let's say that it lasts anywhere between half an hour and an hour, which is a range within which many teachers might operate. Within such a period of time (real life time, that is), the teacher can create a very successful and satisfying learning experience for her class. However, she will have to remember, to use the old adage, to cut her coat according to her cloth. She will have to strike a balance between the pupils' desire to get to the end of the story and her desire to challenge their understanding. Under the constraints of the stand alone lesson, therefore, she has to select a learning area or theme which it is possible for the pupils to explore, with some depth and purpose, within the story of a drama which will need to be concluded in the single session. This is where the episodic structure comes into its own. It allows the teacher to be highly selective is choosing which aspects of the story to develop with the pupils, allowing the story to move forward while still focusing the pupils on the learning area; it enables her to select strategies which will do what she needs them to do, economically, and enables the provision of a structure which sees the story resolved within the real life time constraints of the one-off lesson.

On the other hand, if the teacher is able to develop a process drama over a number of sessions, as in our key examples, then she has the scope to engage the pupils with a learning area which is more wide-ranging, more demanding or more complex. The episodic structure will again facilitate this exploration because its inherent potential for changing time, place, roles and performance form allows for the children's engagement with both the breadth and the depth demanded by such a learning area.

'But you said there were two things'

Yes, and the second one is to do with how the teacher weaves the contributions of the pupils into the drama.

As we have stressed, one of the cornerstones of process drama is the ownership, by pupils, of their learning. This means the teacher must provide a structure in which pupils' contributions to the shaping of the work can be forefronted and acted upon. Within whole-group improvisation with teacher-in-role, the sense of urgency provided by the 'living through' experience coupled with the questioning skills of the teacher (in role) will stimulate a range of responses from the pupils as they struggle with the problems of resolving the dilemma of the drama.

Sharp 'thinking on your feet' skills make it possible for the teacher-in-role to weave in the contributions of the pupils as the drama continues, and many process dramas are, indeed, resolved in this manner. However, if we recognise the value of the episodic form, we can see that a broader range of possibilities become available to class and teacher. It becomes possible to stop the drama and discuss how to turn the pupil response into dramatic action. Preparation can be made, actions 'rehearsed', consequences seen and revisions made in their light. Moreover, the teacher is able to select the most appropriate way of working to enable the pupils to see and feel their ideas realised in action.

'When you talked about the drama learning contract, you mentioned questioning and now you've mentioned it again. Could you say more about this?'

We're sure we all agree that questioning is a key skill for every teacher. Indeed, there are many educationalists who have written in detail and with power and authority about the centrality of the question to the learning process.

As classroom practitioners we know that we need to be subtle in our use of questioning with pupils and recognise the need to employ different types of questions at different times because we require them to serve different purposes in enabling the learning of our pupils. This is equally true within the structure of process drama.

However, all questioning in process drama should be predicated on the understanding that there is, generally speaking, no clearly defined 'right' answer. This is born out of two broader understandings. The first is that all good theatre poses questions rather than provides answers. It holds an aspect of the human condition up for examination and, through the lens of the dramatic context and the interaction of the characters found there, allows our thoughts and feelings to be disturbed as we struggle to find the answers for ourselves. The second is that process drama is a collaborative form in which the teacher and pupils, together, construct the meaning. What follows on from this is that the teacher will have to construct her questions in such a manner that the understanding and experience of her pupils can be heard and their ideas and solutions woven into the fabric of the drama.

'Could you expand on this?'

Well, it might be useful to spend a moment or two looking at the different types of questions which are crucial in facilitating the development of a process drama and the engagement of the pupils with it. Seeing the purposes they serve should make it easier to know which sort of questions to use, and when. We have included examples from both in the 'now time' of the drama and from outside it because the teacher's questioning strategies in both of these situations impact on her chances of building the drama, *together*, with the pupils.

Category— *Questions which*	*Examples*
help define parameters and summarise decisions	
	In the drama 'Are we agreed that we'll all go to Australia?'

Out of the drama
'Do we all agree that when I speak again our drama will have begun?'

These remind the pupils of the drama learning contract and support the pupils in their understanding that process drama is a social form.

ask for information

In the drama
'Does anyone know how to contact the people who live here i the rainforest?'
Out of the drama
'Which strategy should we use to make the next part of the drama happen?'

These remind the pupils that they are involved in a collaboration with their teacher in structuring in the drama.

provide information

In the drama
'How will we get all the other things into the wagon, apart from the mining gear?'
Out of the drama
'Have we thought of all the problems which the lawyers will face?'

These steer the pupils without the teacher imposing her ideas.

challenge the pupils to think more deeply

In the drama
'Has everyone written their last letter home?'
Out of the drama
'How did you feel when you saw the message and realised what it meant?'

These focus the pupils to consider the implications of the drama.

stimulate investigation and research

In the drama
'Do we know exactly what Darwin wrote?'

Out of the drama
'How long would it have taken
a ship to sail to Australia in those days?'

These challenge the pupils to find out information in order that the drama can move on.

offer choices

In the drama
'Should we all go together or split up
now and rendezvous later?'
Out of the drama
'Do you want an imaginary dragon or do
you want me to be the dragon for you?'

These challenge the pupils to make a decision between two courses of action while excluding the possibility of others.

increase tension

In the drama
'Does anyone know how hot it gets
here?'
Out of the drama
'What would you like the next danger to
be?'

These allow the teacher to refocus or increase the tension of the drama.

provide opportunity for reflection

In the drama
'I wonder what made each of us decide
to make this journey?'
Out of the drama
'What sort of person would have stood
up for the others like that?'

These challenge the pupils to think about what the experience means to them.

The structure of many of these questions is designed to be musing, reflective and inviting. They seek to draw the pupils in through more indirect routes which put the teacher firmly in a position of not knowing or of uncertainty. This approach to questioning is firmly related to the status of the role that the teacher takes in the drama. We can see here that a role which does not carry with it the ultimate authority is one which will more readily be able to ask the sorts of questions we have been discussing here. In other words, this combination of TIR status and questioning consequently puts the onus of decision onto the pupils.

Of course, one of the consequences of asking pupils questions to which you really do want them to respond is that you get a host of answers. As we have stressed throughout, process drama actively seeks to involve pupils in shaping the direction of their own learning and as you can see from this brief selection of sample questions the teacher is inviting genuine responses which will help to shape the direction of the drama. However, this also means that action is required of her in order that she fulfils her part of the bargain – the bargain being that to invite pupils to find the solution to the immediate problem at hand, means the teacher has a duty to find the means by which they can see their ideas in action and meet the consequences of them.

This is a key point. Your sophisticated questioning will count for nothing if you hear the pupils' responses and then say, 'but this is what we are going to do'. The pupils will feel cheated and let down and quickly realise that you were not really interested in what they thought, and that you make all the decisions anyway. This slip will undermine your hard work and skill in structuring a drama in which the pupils have been committed and involved.

We realise that for teachers coming newly to process drama it feels 'safer' to have the course of the drama mapped out in complete detail because if feels as if you know exactly what is going to happen at all times. However, if you follow this through into practice, it will mean that the children will not be making any real contribution to what is happening in the drama. They will merely be acting as the puppets while the teacher pulls their strings. In consequence, they will have little sense of ownership about their work and gain relatively little from it.

'So how do you include all the pupils' ideas?'

Well, it's not always going to be possible to do so. There will be times when the pupils have offered downright contradictory suggestions or suggestions which are out of sync with the place and time of the drama. However, the key to success here is making each pupil feel his contribution is *valued* within the framework of the collaborative nature of drama.

We are sure this will not be a new idea to you. As classroom practitioners you will already have a number of strategies which you employ to ensure that the voices of all of your pupils are heard. However, here are a number of strategies which we have found successful:

- recording the pupils' contributions publicly – on paper or a chalkboard, for example – so the whole group can consider all the possibilities;

- sharing ideas with a partner or small group – 'Talk to the botanist near you and see if you can think of a plan' – before presenting it to the rest of the group;
- looking for commonalities in responses and clustering them together.

As we mentioned at the beginning of this section on questioning, a great deal has already been written about the topic. If you would like to find out more, there are a number of texts which have very thorough and clear sections on questioning in drama and you will find details of them at the end of the book in 'Further reading'.

'You've not mentioned monitoring and assessment of progress'

That's true! Our aim has been to focus on the principles of planning process drama in a way which allows this genre to be used within different curricula briefs. However, the clear relationship between progression and assessment and the particular demands of any individual curriculum means that a detailed examination of this important area is beyond the scope of this book. However, there are some key points which we would like to stress.

Firstly, monitoring pupils' progress and assessing their achievement is as important in drama as it is in any other area of the curriculum. There has long been a debate about whether it is possible to assess achievement in the arts and, if it is possible, whether it is desirable. There are those who have argued that the very act of assessment somehow stifles pupils' creativity and undermines the very development that teachers are trying to engender.

We do not subscribe to this view. As teachers, our task is to promote the learning of our pupils and in order to do that we need to know how they are getting on. Furthermore, to ignore the current educational climate, which sees monitoring, assessment, reporting and accountability as key elements of practice, would be foolhardy. Moreover, we think that all teachers recognise the key part assessing achievement plays in the planning process – irrespective of what is being taught. The assessment – planning – teaching – learning loop will be familiar to us all.

So, the critical point, for us, is not whether drama should be assessed, but *how* it should be assessed.

As teachers, we will all be conscious of the need to match assessment methods to the progress and achievement which is to be assessed. But this raises a second, critical point. We need to be clear about *what children may learn* by engaging in drama so that we can identify appropriate methods for assessing it.

Some teachers, those working in Scotland, for example, have an explicit drama curriculum which contains detailed level descriptors of achievement in drama. Others teach in a context where drama is less developed in a national drama curriculum. More may find themselves working within a local or school developed drama curriculum. Others, will find themselves using drama as a methodology within other curriculum subjects.

However, recalling Chapter 1 will remind us of the potential drama offers for learning about the art form and, through the art form, about other things. We identified three broad categories of learning – learning about the art form itself; personal and social learning – including language, spiritual and moral development; and cross-curricular learning. Effective, useful assessment then, needs to take into account the range of learning possibilities. However, the *weighting* that any particular programme will give to each of these areas will depend on the sort of curriculum structure in which the drama is taking place.

However, we think that a further key point lies here. While assessment of pupils' progress in their understanding of, say, conservation issues, evolution or the Australian gold rush, or of their ability to work as team members or to problem-solve, is absolutely appropriate and desirable, assessing the achievement *only* which is content-led or concerned with personal and social development will *not* provide the teacher with an insight into the progress her pupils are making *in drama*. This is really very important. If we accept that developing ability in the art form of drama is not only of value intrinsically, but also that becoming more adept in working in the art form will improve the quality of learning in those areas which spring from working through it, then it becomes clear that monitoring pupil progress in drama is essential. As we pointed out in Chapter 1, the higher the quality of the drama experience, the higher the quality of the learning: and essential to this is the increasing skill, confidence and sophistication with which pupils engage in drama. Assessment of these, then, becomes a key element in the ongoing cycle of teaching and learning.

To put it another way, no matter in which curriculum structure we teach drama, our aim should be to *strike a balance in assessment*, monitoring progress in all three categories of learning.

'What about assessment methods?'

We have already mentioned the need to match methods of assessment to the types of achievement being assessed and once again, the teacher's particular curriculum brief will have an impact here. There are already a number of publications which contain good advice on assessment in clear and informative chapters which we feel are very helpful, and we have included details in the 'Futher reading' section.
In addition, we would suggest bearing the following general points in mind.

When assessing drama the teacher needs to:

- recognise the place and value of drama in her particular curriculum structure;
- develop procedures which are, as far as possible, objective, fair and criteria-referenced;

- recognise the tensions between the social, ephemeral nature of drama and the need to monitor individual progress;
- accommodate different types of learning in drama;
- recognise that the nature of drama means not all learning outcomes in drama are predictable;
- involve pupils in the assessment of their own progress;
- remember that assessment informs future planning.

Useful assessment methods include:

- observation and note-taking by the teacher;
- pupil-kept drama log;
- photographs, audio and video recordings;
- debriefing discussions between peers and with teacher;
- writing and drawing in and out of role.

There is one further point that we should stress here. This particular book is concerned with process drama, but, as we made clear at the very outset, process drama is not the only genre of theatre used within an educational context. Whether following an explicit drama curriculum or using drama in a cross-curricular manner, there are other ways of working, apart from process drama, with which the teacher will need to engage her class from time to time – presentations in assemblies, the study of plays and playwrights, the performance of a play, playwriting, responding to and evaluating drama, physical theatre, puppetry, mime, the craft and technical aspects of theatre, and so on. While all fall under the drama umbrella, each offers a different emphasis of opportunity for pupils; some in what we called Strand A learning and some in Strand B, and assessment processes will need to recognise this. What we must remember is that it is the combination of different ways of working which will meet the demands of a curriculum and that no single way of working is going to serve the needs of all of the pupils all of the time. They need to have the opportunity to engage with a wide spectrum of drama if they are to make progress in the fullest sense.

However, although process drama is not the entirety of drama in an educational context, it is, nonetheless, a central and powerful means by which pupils learn about drama and, through it, about other things.

'And now?'

Have a go at putting it all into practice! What follows next is a planner to help you plan a process drama for you and your class.

CHAPTER 10

Putting it into Practice

In this chapter we hope to give you the opportunity of going through the planning process for yourself.

'But why is there a need for a Planning Chapter – hasn't this whole book been about planning for process drama?'

True, enough! But so far the book has been built around just six key questions. During the course of reading, however, you will have realised that we have raised a number of others. This chapter breaks down the key questions into a series of more specific guiding questions which will help you to be absolutely thorough in your planning. We believe that if you give careful consideration to these, they will serve as a very helpful checklist. If you are able to answer them, then you should be confident that you have brought together the elements needed to provide a meaningful experience for your pupils and yourself.

We urge you to step into the unknown if you have not yet created process drama with your pupils. As we said in the opening chapter, drama is empowering. When teachers exploit drama, they provide a complex, rich and vivid means through which children become artists and, through learning about the art form, develop a means through which to learn about the world around them.

There is, however, one final point to make and it is this...

children find well-constructed drama engaging, exciting, moving, challenging, rewarding and hugely enjoyable.

A Process Drama Planner

Follow the step-by-step sequence to arrive at your plan. Use the sub-questions in each section as a checklist to ensure that you have covered all the planning points. Photocopy the pages and use the grid as a planning sheet.

THEME/LEARNING AREA

Key Question 1

With which area of human experience do I want the pupils to engage and on what specific aspect of this do I want to focus their learning?   **What?**

When deciding on your theme or learning area, remember that learning from drama may be:
- ◊ about the art form of drama
- ◊ personal and social (including language, cultural, moral and spiritual development)
- ◊ cross-curricular
- ◊ that learning about drama and learning through drama are intertwined
- ◊ and that all of this will happen within the framework of your own particular curriculum structure.

Check the following points
- ◊ What opportunities are there for drama/role play in the curriculum you are following?
- ◊ How much flexibility do you have in choosing themes?
- ◊ Is your learning area/theme closely related to some area of human experience? If so, what?
- ◊ If the theme is not directly related to an area of human experience, how will you connect it to **people** and their experiences?
- ◊ Are there opportunities for cross-curricular learning: personal, social, moral, cultural and spiritual learning and learning about the art form of drama?

Review Chapter 3 for more help in deciding what you want your pupils to learn about

My chosen learning area(s) for this drama is/are:

CONTEXT

Key Question 2

Which particular circumstances will be created by the drama to explore the theme?   **Where?**
When?

When deciding on your dramatic context, remember that:
- ◊ drama is a powerful means through which to contextualise learning
- ◊ you need to take into consideration the real life context in which you and your pupils are working
- ◊ dramatic contexts can be located in the past, present or future.

Check the following points
- ◊ Have you considered the number/age/social health of your class?
- ◊ Do you have a special room or space for drama, or will you have to work in the classroom?
- ◊ Are you able to rearrange furniture or will you have to work with it 'in situ'?
- ◊ Do you have the resources you need?
- ◊ What range of possible fictional circumstances have you thought of in which to explore the theme?
- ◊ Which of these will best serve your particular class?
- ◊ Will your chosen dramatic context provide opportunities for specific contextualisation of learning: e.g., oral language – technical or professional; written language – letters, reports, petitions; research, experimentation; new performance forms?

Review Chapter 4 for more help in deciding on the dramatic context

My chosen dramatic context is:

ROLE

Key Question 3
Who are the pupils and the teacher going to be in the drama?

Who?

When deciding on the roles in the drama, remember that:
◊ children almost always take on adult roles in their own dramatic playing
◊ at least at the outset, roles bound together through common interest are most enabling of the drama
◊ teacher-in-role is a powerful means of enabling the drama.

Check the following points
- pupils' roles
◊ Is it likely that the roles you have selected would be found in the context you have chosen?
◊ Do the roles have a common interest in the circumstances of the drama?
◊ Are there opportunities for individual identities to be developed within the group?
◊ Are there likely to be opportunities for a range of opinions to be developed within the dramatic circumstances?
◊ Might the pupils be expected to change roles during the course of the drama?
◊ How experienced are the pupils in taking a role, and might they need to practice first?
- teacher-in-role
◊ How comfortable and experienced are you in using TIR?
◊ Have you planned to change roles in the drama?
◊ If not, how prepared are you to do so if the circumstances of the drama require it?
◊ What relationship will there be between the TIR and the roles of the pupils: e.g., authority role, colleague, devil's advocate, messenger?
◊ What will be the resulting status of your role in relation to those of the pupils?
◊ Will your role be able to model behaviour, attitude and language for the pupils to help them develop their roles?

Review Chapter 5 for more help in deciding on the roles of the pupils and teacher-in-role

My chosen role for the pupil is:

My chosen TIR is:

FRAME

Key Question 4
Which viewpoint will the roles have in order to create tension in the drama and how distanced do the roles need to be?

When deciding on the frame for the drama remember that: # Why?
◊ frame creates dramatic tension to provide an imperative for action
◊ the communication function of frame creates collective concern and the imperative for talk
◊ the distancing function protects into experience.

Check the following points
◊ What point of view will the roles have (both TIR and pupils) about the event or situation being developed in the drama?
◊ What, exactly, is it that will give tension to the situation and help develop points of view?
◊ What kind of collective concern might the role be expected to develop in the dramatic context of drama?
◊ To what extent will the roles be empowered to do something about their situation in the drama?
◊ How distanced by time and/or relationship are the roles from the main area of exploration?
◊ What opportunities will exist for the pupils to deepen their investment in the unfolding situation of the drama?
◊ Do you envisage opportunities for re-framing the roles by shifting their point of view?
◊ Have you ensured sufficient protection for the pupils in relation to the subject matter and the experience of the drama?

Review Chapter 6 for more help in deciding on the frame of the drama

My chosen frame for drama is:

SIGN

Key Question 5

What artefacts, personal items, sounds and so on, will I need to bring significance to the drama?

How?

When deciding on the signs for the drama, remember that:
there are three aspects to planning sign
◊ signs which 'hook' the pupils into drama
◊ other prepared signs which bring significance by focusing attention on the theme or learning area
◊ teacher's sign which supports the teacher-in-role.

Check the following points

◊ What will you use to 'hook' the pupils into drama – a notice, map, object, sound?
◊ What other prepared sign might you need to have ready as the drama begins to unfold – a scroll, doctor's bag, a jewel?
◊ What things do you need as TIR to sign and 'reinforce' your role in the drama – item of costume, prop?
◊ Will you need to prepare items to sign the pupils' roles – badges of office?
◊ Will the pupils in role make anything to help establish the drama?
◊ Will you use sign to indicate 'absent others' – symbolically, iconically, expressively?
◊ Is the signing going to be culturally appropriate for the pupils and clear?

Review Chapter 7 for more help in deciding on the sign for the drama

My chosen signs are:

STRATEGIES

Key Question 6

Which ways of working will I use, in which combination, for what purpose?

How?

When deciding on the strategies you are going to use in the drama, remember that:
◊ whole-group improvisation with teacher-in-role is a central strategy but there are many more
◊ there are different types of strategy which serve different purposes in developing the drama
◊ it is important to choose the strategy which will create that part of the drama most 'meaningfully'.

Check the following points

◊ Do you have sufficient strategies in your repertoire to start? Make a note of the ones with which you are comfortable.
◊ Do you have sufficient strategies to provide you with alternative ways of proceeding and to introduce new strategies to the pupils?
◊ Are there any strategies which you are overusing? Remember, one of your aims is to introduce pupils to a range of performance forms.
◊ Will the pupils have the opportunity to suggest which strategies might be used to move the drama forward?
◊ Are the strategies being used, culturally appropriate to the pupils involved? Are you drawing on performance forms from the pupils' tradition?
◊ Are the strategies appropriate to the learning needs of the pupils?
◊ Are you thinking ahead about how the drama might unfold, and planning strategies which might be introduced later?
◊ Have you chosen strategies which are appropriate to the material being explored? Are they helping to deepen the experience for the pupils and encouraging reflection on the drama?

Review Chapter 9 for more help in deciding on the strategies for the drama

My chosen strategies for the drama are:

Finally –

◇ Have you negotiated a drama learning contract with the class?
◇ Does everyone understand what the perameters are?
◇ Have you agreed signals for starting and stopping the drama?
◇ Are you clear about the subtle questioning you will need to use?
◇ Do you remember that process drama works well as an episodic form?
◇ Are you willing to offer the pupils the opportunity to contribute to the shape and direction of their learning, and ready to weave their ideas into the drama?
◇ Have you given thought to assessment opportunities inside and outside the drama?
◇ Do you remember that drama is powerful and also FUN?

Review Chapter 9 to get more help

You are ready to shift into 'now time' and begin!

CHAPTER 11

Further Reading/Bibliography

Further reading

We have tried to provide a comprehensive guide to the planning of process drama. However, it is clear that no single publication can hope to cover every aspect of a subject in complete detail. There are other practitioners who have written on the subject of process drama and, of course, broader aspects of drama within an educational setting. What follows is a list of titles (in alphabetical order) which will be useful if you would like to delve into process drama more deeply or to explore the broader spectrum of drama within educational settings. Some focus on drama in the early years, some on the primary years and some on the secondary years. There are also others which are cross phase.

Beginning Drama 4–11, Winston, J. and Tandy, M., 1998, David Fulton Publishers. A clear and encouraging book for those beginning drama with early years and primary pupils. It places drama within the curriculum and school context and has a particularly helpful chapter on continuity, progression and assessment. An updated second edition is now available.

Beginning Drama 11–14, Neelands, J., 1998, David Fulton Publishers. Provides positive support to teachers new to drama. It gives a clear indication of what they need to know, understand and be able to do. Good sections on progression and assessment.

Drama – A handbook for primary teachers, Readman, G. and Lamont, G., 1994, BBC Education. This is an extremely clear, easy to read text which has lots of practical examples and a particularly good section on progression and assessment.

Drama and Traditional Story in the Early Years, Toye, N. and Prendiville, P., 2000, Routledge. A stimulating account of drama in the early years, which provides a wide range of examples supported by a clear rationale. A good section on assessment, recording and progression.

The Drama Box and Drama Book, Baldwin, P. and Hendy, L.,1994, Collins. A collection of materials for primary drama with a very good and informative book, which combines practice with theory.

Drama for Learning: Dorothy Heathcote's Mantle of the Expert Approach to Education, Heathcote, D. and Bolton, G., 1995, Heinemann. A key text about the work of a key practitioner. It explores a seminal way of working within process drama. It really does represent one avenue of process drama in its most fully developed form.

Drama Structures, O'Neill, C. and Lambert, A., 1982, Heinemann. A stalwart text, which offers a series of well-constructed dramas, together with key teaching skills and methods.

Drama Worlds, O'Neill, C., 1995, Heinemann. This book is for those who wish to delve more deeply into the theory of process drama and its place as a genre of theatre. It also contains clear accounts of dramas which exemplify the text.

Making Sense of Drama: a guide to classroom practice, Neelands, J., 1984, Heinemann. This book remains very relevent for teachers approaching process drama. It has a particularly good section on questioning.

Practical Primary Drama, Davis, G., 1983, Heinemann. Although written some time ago, this is a very accessible text and its guidance remains of help to both students and inexperienced teachers of drama.

The Process of Drama: Negotiating Art and Meaning, O'Toole, J., 1992, Routledge. This is another text which, although challenging, provides the means to engage with the rationale and philosophy of process drama.

Progression in Secondary Drama, Kempe, A. and Ashwell, M., 2000, Heinemann. As the title suggests, this up to the minute book provides a thorough examination of progression in drama at the secondary level.

Starting Drama Teaching, Fleming, M., 1998, David Fulton Publishers. This is required reading for drama teachers. It is thoughtful, considered and gives a firm foundation to teaching drama, combining theory and practice.

Stimulating Drama: Cross-curricular Approaches to Drama in the Primary School, Baldwin, P., 1992, National Drama Publications. Contains a set of lessons, described clearly and in a very practical way.

Structuring Drama Work, Neelands, J. and Goode, T., 2000, Cambridge University Press. This is the revised and expanded version of Jonothan Neelands' classic text, which defines a wide range of drama strategies/theatre conventions and provides principles for structuring drama work and drama-based learning.

Teaching Drama: a mind of many wonders ..., Morgan, N. and Saxton, J., 1984, Hutchinson. This is another must read for drama teachers. It is comprehensive, accessibly written and provides a clear framework for drama. It has particularly useful sections on both questioning and assessment.

The Teaching of Drama in the Primary School, Woolland, B., 1993, Longman. An established text with a good section on questioning.

Journals
Articles and papers of interest can be found in these regularly published journals.

Drama and *Drama Research,* both published by National Drama Publications, the publishing wing of National Drama, the leading professional association for drama educators in the UK.

Research in Drama Education, published by Carfax.

Drama Australia and *The Australian Drama Education Magazine,* both published by Drama Australia, the Australian drama teachers' association.

NZADIE Journal, published by the New Zealand Association for Drama in Education, the New Zealand drama teachers' association.

Websites
The following websites will be of interest.

National Drama   www.nationaldrama.co.uk
International Drama/Theatre in Education Association
www.educ.queensu.ca/~idea/
DramaWest   http://members.iinet.net.au/~kimbo2/Dramawest/
Drama Australia   www.dramaaustralia.org.au/
New Zealand Association for Drama in Education   www.nzadie.org.nz/

American Alliance for Theatre and Education   www.aate.com/
Council for Drama and Dance Education (a Canadian site)
http://members.home.net/4drama/

Bibliography

Bruner, J. (1966) *Towards a Theory of Instruction.* USA: Harvard University Press.

Heathcote, D. (1995) *Pieces of Dorothy,* videotape. University of Newcastle upon Tyne.

Neelands, J. and Goode, T. (2000) *Structuring Drama Work.* Cambridge University Press.

Pierce, C. S. cited in Noth, W. (1990) *The Handbook of Semiotics.* USA: Indiana University Press.

Toye, N. and Prendiville, P. (2000) *Drama and Traditional Story in the Early Years.* London: Routledge.

Index

Printed in the United Kingdom
by Lightning Source UK Ltd.
133144UK00006B/95-100/A